M000036196

Going GLOBAL

Beyond the Boundaries

The Role of the Black Church
in the Great Commission of Jesus Christ

Denise K. Gates, Writer
Carl F. Ellis Jr., Editor

Urban Ministries, Inc.

Urban Ministries, Inc.
The African American Christian Publishing
& Communications Co

Writer: Denise K. Gates

Publisher
UMI (Urban Ministries, Inc.)
P. O. Box 436987
Chicago, IL 60643-6987

First Edition
First Printing
ISBN: 0-940955-95-4

1-800-860-8642
www.urbanministries.com

Printed in the United States of America.

Table of Contents

Preface

One morning, a woman called in to a radio talk show and said that she could not possibly believe in a God who would allow the kind of injustice, suffering, and tragedy that seems to be everywhere you look today. "Besides," she continued, "what kind of God would be so barbaric as to allow His Son to be beaten, suffer, and die so horrifically?"

If she were speaking to you, how would you respond?

The Bible says that when Adam and Eve sinned, the earth itself changed (Genesis 3). Instead of working for them, the soil seemed to work against them in a profuse production of weeds. As a result, they had to "toil" to get the harvest that they had once effortlessly enjoyed. The effect of sin is also evident in the human heart. Much of the suffering we experience comes by the hands of sinful people. Unfortunately, there are people who look at the things humanity has done, and they turn away from God.

What a testimony African Americans can give to the world! The Declaration of Independence states that all men are created equal, but this has not been our experience. We have suffered much, endured much, and overcome much. African Americans have been owned as property, counted as three-fifths of a person; lynched without legal action or public outcry; and treated as second-class citizens with few rights and fewer opportunities for much of our history in this country.

However, the truth remains that God can cause all things to work together for good for those who love Him and are called according to His purpose (Romans 8:28). Our past and current experiences can serve a great purpose when we proclaim the truth of the Word and point to the sustaining hand of God.

Purpose of the Book. *Going Global—Beyond the Boundaries: The Role of the Black Church in the Great Commission of Jesus Christ* provides a unique perspective of the role of the African American church in African American history. Although the church has always been our foundation, political and social history often overshadows the theological aspects behind the things that occur. Thus, the focus of this study is not on personal or social issues but on how the African American church has impacted our culture. The book reveals our historic role in global missions, especially missions to

Africa, and presents a call to return to the place where the African American church is a force in our culture and active in our world.

The Leader's Guide. This leader's guide is designed for leaders who use *Going Global—Beyond the Boundaries* as a text for group Bible studies, retreats, Sunday School electives, Vacation Bible School courses, Christian Education Congresses, or Black history studies. It contains a suggested lesson plan, Life Application questions, Bible Application exercises, Personal Application questions, and Going Global questions that relate to each chapter of the book.

The leader's guide also provides lesson objectives, directions for group study, and answers to the Bible Application exercises. Each chapter includes:

- An opening Scripture verse that is studied by all age groups following UMIs Vacation Bible School 2005 curriculum
- Chapter topics and definitions to facilitate a review and discussion of the book in a group setting
- Open-ended Life Application questions that relate the content of the book to the Word of God and the experience of the participants
- Bible Application exercises and answers that enable participants to explore what God's Word reveals about the role of the African American church and the importance of missions
- Personal Application questions that encourage participants to apply the Word of God to their attitudes and activities
- Going Global questions at the end of each chapter that challenge participants to examine their level of missionary involvement and act upon the information and the truths they have learned

These exercises and questions can be transferred to overhead transparencies to facilitate group discussion, be given as take home assignments, or be used in daily devotions.

The Student Workbook. A separate student workbook also accompanies the book, *Going Global—Beyond the Boundaries*. The student workbook provides a place for students to record their answers to the Life Application questions, Bible Application exercises, Personal Application questions, and

Going Global questions. You may also encourage participants to use the space in the back of their student workbook to jot down their thoughts and insights about each chapter.

Leading the Discussion. Effective leadership always requires good preparation. Begin by reading *Going Global—Beyond the Boundaries* from beginning to end. Take notes on each chapter, underline interesting ideas, and write down related thoughts or remembered experiences that can be used as illustrations or examples.

Then survey the entire leader's guide. Knowing the objectives and topics of the Bible study will help you conduct the lesson effectively. If questions arise about topics that will be covered later, you may choose to postpone the discussion until that time. Also, feel free to modify the Bible study session to meet the needs and time restraints of your particular group.

Before each Bible study session:

1. Pray for wisdom.
2. Know the goal.
3. Depend on the Holy Spirit
4. Study the material to be covered. Review the content of the chapter and all of the information in the leader's guide.
5. Contact participants before the first session to see if they have obtained a copy of the book and workbook for this study.
6. Encourage participants to read each chapter before the meeting and use the space in the back of the student workbook to briefly note the ideas or information that they want to remember.
7. Gather your notes and any supplies needed to facilitate the discussion. If you will use overhead transparencies, make copies of the Life Application questions, Chapter Review topics, and the Words You Should Know to facilitate discussion. If you plan to use a chalkboard or newsprint to display questions or record answers, gather these supplies as well.
8. Prepare the space by setting up refreshments for participants, arranging chairs in a semicircle, etc.

During the session:

1. Begin with prayer.
2. Maintain a relaxed, informal atmosphere.
3. Keep track of the time.
4. Encourage "down to earth" discussion (discourage intellectualizing).
5. Be sure to focus on biblical truths.

Finally, be yourself! You don't have to become the "expert." Keep in mind that this is not your Bible study—it is God's. Relax and enjoy studying and applying God's Word with fellow believers in Christ.

Introduction

God is at work in our lives, our communities, our culture, and our world.

His work did not just begin, nor will it end, with us. It was God's plan from the beginning that through Jesus all the nations of the earth would be blessed (Genesis 22:18; 1 Peter 1:20). While we have the opportunity, we must do our part. We have a purpose, and we play an important part in the plan of God.

To participate in the work of God in the world today, we must ask ourselves, "What is God's work?" and "What part am I called to play?" Too many people receive salvation and become satisfied. Is that the outcome that God has planned? Or would He have us to do as Jesus did—go out to bring salvation to the lost as ministers of the truth, healing, and help that is at the very core of the Gospel?

We truly are those who possess Good News. To overcome the problems that are so pervasive in the world today, we have a living hope. To meet the overwhelming needs, we have God's power. To conquer the works of darkness and turn back the tide of wickedness, we have been given mighty spiritual weapons. We have been equipped to do the work of God in the earth. We are God's workmanship, and we have been created to do good works (Ephesians 2:10).

The Great Commission has been given. It is our time to "go and make disciples" (Matthew 28:19–20). This is our time to make a difference for the glory of God and facilitate God's salvation and deliverance in our generation.

However, before we go, there are things we should know. The Bible tells us that people perish because of their lack of knowledge (Hosea 4:6). Using God's perspective, we can know:

- who we are (identity),
- from whence we have come (history),
- what we have endured (testimony), and
- where we are going (direction and destiny).

Going Global—Beyond the Boundaries provides biblical information in a historical and cultural context to help African Americans become more effective witnesses in the world today. This study will examine and answer some critical questions and enable you to gain a new or renewed perspective on the role of missions in the African American church and in the lives of our people.

In spite of Satan's best efforts to steal, kill, and destroy, we have endured, we have stood, and still we rise! Let us do our part to bring to our generation the truth of God's Word—the Good News of the Gospel—and the demonstrated evidence of the power of God at work in the lives of His people.

Chapter 1

Unashamed of the Gospel

Format for Sessions of 90 Minutes or More

PART ONE		PART TWO	
MIN.	ACTIVITY	MIN.	ACTIVITY
5	Prayer	20	Small Group Study
10	Introduction	15	Small Group Presentations
15	Chapter Review	15	Large Group Presentations
20	Life Application Discussion	5	Going Global Commitment
		5	Prayer

For sessions of less than 90 minutes, use PART ONE only and assign the Bible Application exercises as homework. Read the Going Global exercise at the end of the study aloud, and encourage participants to come prepared to share their results next week. Then close the class in prayer.

*To complete the group study in PART TWO, each participant will need a copy of the student workbook that accompanies the book, *Going Global—Beyond the Boundaries.*

Lesson Aim: At the end of this two-part session, the participants should: (a) realize that the beauty of our African American identity is rooted in the fact that we are in God's image; (b) recognize that the Word of God speaks to every cultural and historical situation; (c) know that the Gospel is God's power for salvation of everyone who believes; and (d) make a commitment to share the Gospel with others and apply God's Word to every area of life.

Key Verse: "I am not ashamed of the gospel, because it is the power of God for the salvation of everyone who believes: first for the Jew, then for the Gentile" (Romans 1:16, NIV).

Lesson Focus: Through His death, resurrection, and ascension, Jesus brought our salvation not only so that we would be able to go to heaven, but also so that we would be agents of God's kingdom. Therefore, we bring God's grace, love, and power to others in Jesus' name.

PART ONE
Prayer
Open the session with prayer, including the lesson aim.

Introduction
In the first session, invite the participants to introduce themselves. Then share your excitement, expectations, or hopes for this Bible study.

Ask them to read the Key Verse aloud in unison. This verse appears at the beginning of chapter 1 in their workbooks. Then ask them to silently read the focus statement that follows this verse. If there are participants who do not have workbooks, read this statement aloud to the group.

Chapter Review
Use the following topics to review and discuss chapter 1.

- Definition of Theology
- Cultural Distinctions of African American Theology
- Life Application of Biblical Truth
- What is the Gospel?
- Sharing the Gospel of Jesus Christ

You may write these topics on the chalkboard or newsprint, or uncover them one at a time using an overhead projector and transparencies. Try to limit the discussion to five minutes or less for each topic.

Words You Should Know
It is often useful to define the terms that are discussed to ensure that the group shares a common understanding. Read or display the following definitions and allow a few minutes for questions or comments.

- **Theology**—The study of the nature of God and the relationship of the human and divine. In this chapter it is defined as the application of God's Word to every area of life.

- **Epistemology**—The study of the origin, nature, and limits of human knowledge (what we should know about God).

- **Ethics**—A set of moral principles (how we should obey God).

- **Western (White) theology**—To counter the challenge of unbelieving philosophy and science, it was mostly concerned with what we should know about God (based on philosophy and theoretical knowledge).

- **African American theology**—To counter the challenge of oppressive slavery and racism, it was mostly concerned with how we should obey God (based on concepts of right and wrong).

- **Preaching the Gospel**—Proclaiming the Good News of salvation available through Jesus Christ; teaching people how to avail themselves of God's offer of salvation; declaring all of the truths, precepts, and promises of Christianity; and witnessing in word and deeds through the power of the Holy Spirit.

Life Application Questions

Ask the participants to review and share their answers to the following Life Application questions:

- Why is the knowledge of who we are and whose we are so important?
- Why is the African American theological perspective unique?
- Why is the Word of God able to address our unique situation?
- Why should we share the Gospel?

These Life Application questions also appear in the student workbook with space to record their answers. You can ask the participants to take a few minutes to answer these questions. Or you can read the questions aloud or display them to facilitate discussion. You may also wish to share your point of view as a fellow participant in Bible study.

PART TWO
Small Group Study

Separating Small Groups. Ask the participants to form three small groups. Each group will study a different set of questions and report their findings to the larger group at the end of the study period. Assign the Bible Application exercises as follows:

Group #1   Created in God's Image
Group #2   Not Ashamed in His Presence
Group #3   Not Ashamed of the Gospel

Feel free to tailor the small group study to fit the size and needs of your class. If your study group is small, you may focus on Bible Application exercise #3.

Set a Time Limit. About 15–20 minutes should be sufficient. Check the clock to determine how much time is available. Then notify the groups of the time that they should reconvene.

Sharing Insights. Encourage the small group members to vary their study methods. For example, the participants could locate different verses and take turns reading them aloud to the group. Then they could spend a few minutes discussing the answers to the questions. Or the group could divide the time in half. During the first part they each could read and answer all of the assigned questions. Then they would come together to discuss their answers and share insights and opinions. Remind them to include a discussion of the Personal Application questions as part of their study.

Preparing Reports. Have each small group select the participant(s) who will take notes, summarize the discussion, and present the group's findings.

Large Group Discussion
Reconvene the Group. Call the small groups back together.

Present Small Group Reports. Have the selected participants report the results of their small group study. Encourage the other groups to take notes, and allow time for discussion and questions within the larger group.

Monitor the Time. Remind the representatives to try to summarize the small group's discussion in two or three minutes. Allocate up to three minutes to discuss each group's presentation.

Going Global Commitment
Read the Going Global exercise aloud to the group. Then give the participants a few minutes to answer the question and make a personal commitment. Encourage them to come prepared to share their results next week.

Closing
Ask the participants to read chapter 2 of *Going Global—Beyond the Boundaries* and record their notes at the end of their student workbooks.

Remind them to bring their Bibles and workbooks to the next session. Close the class with prayer focused on the lesson aim.

Bible Application Exercises and Answers
1. Created in God's Image
You are "fearfully and wonderfully made" (Psalm 139:14). Your African American identity is part of the plan and intent of God. The Creator of all diversity, from the microscopic to the immeasurable, has created you in His image in order that you might know and worship Him.

Review the following verses, and restate their truths in your own words. Make your statements personal. Write as if God is speaking directly to you and about you, because He is.

a. Genesis 1:26–27

God made me in His image and likeness. His desire is that I would have dominion over all the earth and everything in it.

b. Psalm 100:3

I must know and remember that God is God. He has made me, so I don't have to make something of myself or define myself by myself. I belong to God, and He cares for me.

c. Psalm 139:14

I will praise God because I am fearfully and wonderfully made.

d. Isaiah 43:1–2

God has created and redeemed me. He calls me by name, and I am His. He has promised to protect and preserve me. Though I may face life's difficulties, God causes me to prevail.

e. 2 Corinthians 5:17–18

God has made me a new creature in Christ Jesus. I am His child, and He has given me the ministry of reconciliation to encourage others to become part of the family of God.

f. Ephesians 2:10

I am God's masterpiece. I have a unique purpose. I was created to do the good works that God has planned for me to do.

▼▲▼▲▼▲▼▲▼▲▼▲▼▲▼▲▼▲▼▲▼▲▼▲▼▲▼▲▼▲

Personal Application

How should knowing your God-given identity affect the way that you act and think?

Answers will vary.

How can the knowledge that you are created in God's image anchor you in the face of poverty, racism, or injustice?

Answers will vary.

2. Not Ashamed in His Presence

Adam and Eve were created to be in personal relationship with God. Before they disobeyed God, they were naked and not ashamed. After they sinned, they were ashamed and they hid from God. However, we know that nothing is hidden from God. Hebrews 4:13 (KJV) says, "Neither is there any creature that is not manifest in his sight: but all things are naked and opened unto the eyes of him with whom we have to do."

Read the following verses and record how you can keep yourself from being ashamed in the presence of the Lord.

a. Psalm 25:2–3

Trust in the Lord and wait on Him.

b. Psalm 119:6

Obey God's commands.

c. Psalm 119:46

Give your personal testimony of God's goodness.

d. Psalm 119:80

Treasure God's Word in your heart.

e. Isaiah 50:7

Be determined to do God's will

f. Romans 5:5

Hope in God.

g. Romans 10:11

Believe on Jesus Christ.

h. 2 Timothy 2:15
> Study God's Word.

i. 1 John 2:28
> Abide in Christ.

Personal Application

"Those who look to him are radiant; their faces are never covered with shame" (Psalm 34:5). List three practical ways that you can "look to the Lord" on a daily basis.
> Answers will vary.

Jesus said, "If anyone is ashamed of me and my words in this adulterous and sinful generation, the Son of Man will be ashamed of him when he comes in his Father's glory with the holy angels" (Mark 8:38). Identify three things that you can do to ensure that you do not become ashamed of your faith in Christ or your trust in God's Word.
> Answers will vary.

3. Not Ashamed of the Gospel

The Gospel is the saving work of God through His Son, Jesus Christ, and a call to faith in Him. This Good News is more than a promise of future salvation. It is an invitation to enter into a real–time relationship with God, which has been God's intention and desire for us from the beginning.

Fill in the blanks below to identify to whom the Gospel should be preached.

> a. "And this gospel of the kingdom will be preached **in the whole world as a testimony to all nations"** (Matthew 24:14).

> b. "Therefore go and **make disciples of all nations,** baptizing them in the name of the Father and of the Son and of the Holy Spirit" (Matthew 28:19).

> c. "And the gospel must first be **preached to all nations"** (Mark 13:10).

> d. "He said to them, 'Go into all the world and **preach the good news to all creation'"** (Mark 16:15).

Use Romans 1:16 to identify the following facts about God's Good News for us.

a. The Person of the Gospel   Jesus Christ

b. The Power of God   the Gospel

c. The Purpose of the Gospel   salvation

d. The People to Whom the Gospel Is Sent   everyone

e. The Method of Acceptance   belief

Personal Application

The Gospel is God's grace and love in action to bring people to Himself. It reveals how:

- God planned our salvation,
- Jesus came to save us, and
- the Holy Spirit works in and through those who believe.

How has the power of the Gospel been demonstrated in your life?
Answers will vary.

Going Global

The Great Commission has been given to every believer. We are called to participate in preaching the Gospel and sharing the Good News of salvation available through Jesus Christ.

List the names of five people that you know who need salvation.
Answers will vary.

Make a commitment to pray for them this week, and be prepared to share your testimony with them if you have an opportunity.

Chapter 2

Suffering and the South

Format for Sessions of 90 Minutes or More

PART ONE		PART TWO	
MIN.	ACTIVITY	MIN.	ACTIVITY
5	Prayer	20	Small Group Study
10	Going Global Discussion	15	Small Group Presentations
15	Introduction	15	Large Group Presentations
20	Chapter Review	5	Going Global Commitment
20	Life Application Discussion	5	Prayer

For sessions of less than 90 minutes, use PART ONE only and assign the Bible Application exercises as homework. Read the Going Global exercise at the end of the study aloud, and encourage the participants to come prepared to share their results next week. Then close the class in prayer.

*To complete the group study in PART TWO, each participant will need a copy of the student workbook that accompanies the book, *Going Global—Beyond the Boundaries.*

Lesson Aim: At the end of this two-part session, the participants should: (a) recognize the distinction between biblical Christianity and man-made religion or distortions of God's Word; (b) relate how the experience of slavery and the fight for civil rights impacted the African American theological perspective; (c) explain why Christianity is cross-cultural and the Gospel is not limited by skin color or social class; and (d) share a testimony of how faith in Christ can sustain us in times of hardship or suffering.

Key Verse: "All the prophets testify about him that everyone who believes in him receives forgiveness of sins through his name" (Acts 10:43, NIV).

Lesson Focus: When our suffering is placed in the hand of God, it will serve a higher purpose. God can take suffering and use it to bring redemption and transformation. He can even use our experience of persecution and affliction to create in us perseverance, endurance, and a quality of faith that is more precious than gold.

PART ONE
Prayer

Open the session with prayer, including the lesson aim.

Going Global Discussion

Invite the participants to share the results of their Going Global commitment from last week's Bible study.

Introduction

Ask the participants to read the Key Verse aloud in unison. This verse appears at the beginning of chapter 2 in their workbooks. Then ask them to silently read the focus statement that follows this verse. If there are participants who do not have workbooks, read this statement aloud to the group.

Chapter Review

Use the following topics to review and discuss chapter 2.

- Christianity and "Christianity-ism"
- The Theology of Suffering
- Suffering and Slavery
- Freedom and Deliverance

You may write these topics on the chalkboard or newsprint, or uncover them one at a time using an overhead projector and transparencies. Try to limit the discussion to five minutes or less for each topic.

Words You Should Know

It is often useful to define the terms that are discussed to ensure that the group shares a common understanding. Read or display the following definitions and allow a few minutes for questions or comments.

- **Christianity**—The system of beliefs and practices based on the Old Testament and the identity, life, and teachings of Jesus in the New Testament, emphasizing Jesus' role as Savior and Lord.

- **Christianity-ism**—A negative form of religion that seeks to impose its own agenda in order to manipulate others. Although it uses the same terminology as Christianity, its motivation and application are often in conflict with the true practice of God's Word.

- **Theology of suffering**—A historic approach to faith in God based on the Old Testament experience of the Israelites in Egypt who gained freedom from slavery and oppression through God's intervention.

- **Paradigm**—A clear example or pattern.

Life Application Questions

Ask the participants to review and share their answers to the following Life Application questions:

- Why is true Christianity cross-cultural?
- Why do true expressions of Christianity (such as styles of worship, prayer, etc.) vary from culture to culture?
- What forms of "Christianity-ism" should the church be on guard against today?
- How did the church serve as a place of refuge for African American slaves?
- What role should the church serve in the culture today?

These Life Application questions also appear in the student workbook with space to record their answers. You can ask the participants to take a few minutes to answer these questions. Or you can read the questions aloud or display them to facilitate discussion. You may also wish to share your point of view as a fellow participant in Bible study.

PART TWO
Small Group Study

Separating Small Groups. Ask the participants to form four small groups. Each group will study a different set of questions and report their findings to the larger group at the end of the study period.

Assign the Bible Application exercises as follows:

Group #1	An Old Testament View of Deliverance
Group #2	A New Testament View of Salvation
Group #3	A New Testament Perspective of Suffering
Group #4	Cross-Cultural Christianity

Feel free to tailor the small group study to fit the size and needs of your class. If your study group is small, you may focus on Bible Application exercises #3 and #4.

Set a Time Limit. About 15-20 minutes should be sufficient. Check the clock to determine how much time is available. Then notify the groups of the time that they should reconvene.

Sharing Insights. Encourage the small group members to vary their study methods. For example, the participants could locate different verses and take turns reading them aloud to the group. Then they could spend a few minutes discussing the answers to the questions. Or the group could divide the time in half. During the first part they each could read and answer all of the assigned questions. Then they would come together to discuss their answers and share insights and opinions. Remind them to include a discussion of the Personal Application questions as part of their study.

Preparing Reports. Have each small group select the participant(s) who will take notes, summarize the discussion, and present the group's findings.

Large Group Discussion
Reconvene the Group. Call the small groups back together.

Present Small Group Reports. Have the selected participants report the results of their small group study. Encourage the other groups to take notes, and allow time for discussion and questions within the larger group.

Monitor the Time. Remind the representatives to try to summarize the small group's discussion in two or three minutes. Allocate up to three minutes to discuss each group's presentation.

Going Global Commitment
Read the Going Global exercise aloud to the group. Then give the participants a few minutes to answer the question and challenge to make a personal commitment to place their hope and trust in Christ in every situation. Encourage them to share their testimonies next week.

Closing
Ask the participants to read chapter 3 of *Going Global—Beyond the Boundaries* and record their notes at the end of their student workbooks. Remind them to bring their Bibles and workbooks to the next session. Close the class with prayer focused on the lesson aim.

Bible Application Exercises and Answers

1. An Old Testament View of Deliverance

African Americans in the South developed a theology of suffering and hope of salvation that was based on the Old Testament experience of the Israelites in the book of Exodus. Exodus 5:1–15:21 recounts the story of people who were enslaved and suffering from economic and political bondage.

Read Exodus 14:13. Describe the type of salvation that Moses expected.
> Moses expected God's divine intervention and direct deliverance from the Egyptians.

Read Moses' song of praise in Exodus 15:1–13. Describe the type of salvation that the Lord provided.
> The Israelites cried out to God for help, and He responded by crushing their opponents and leading them into freedom.

How does the Exodus paradigm relate to the African American southern theology of suffering and hope of salvation?
> This biblical example functioned as a paradigm for African Americans who called upon God to free them as He freed the Israelites in the Exodus account.

Personal Application

Malachi 3:6 assures us that the Lord does not change, and Hebrews 13:8 reminds us that Jesus Christ is the same yesterday, today, and forever. How can you use these truths to sustain you when you need the Lord's direct intervention in your difficult circumstances?
> Answers will vary.

2. A New Testament View of Salvation

In the Old Testament, the word *salvation* usually referred to deliverance from evil or danger. In the New Testament, our understanding of salvation expands to include God's deliverance from the guilt and penalty of sin through the work of Jesus Christ.

Read the verses below and summarize what they reveal about the salvation that God has provided.

a. John 3:17
> God sent His Son so that the world might be saved through Him.

b. Acts 4:12

There is salvation in the name of Jesus; there is no other
name under heaven by which men and women can be saved.

c. Hebrews 5:9

Jesus is the author of eternal salvation for those who obey
and believe in Him.

d. Hebrews 7:25

Jesus is able to save to the uttermost all who come to God
through Him.

Personal Application

Read Hebrews 2:1–3. How can you avoid letting the Word of God "slip"
and neglecting your salvation?

Answers will vary.

3. A New Testament Perspective of Suffering

Although African Americans currently do not experience the same sufferings as our forebears, racism and injustice is part of the daily experience of many. Our walk with Christ will not prevent suffering. But when
we choose to follow Him, we can be confident that we will not go
through our trials alone.

Match the following verses with what they reveal about the believer's
experience of suffering.

a. John 16:33
b. Romans 8:18
c. 2 Timothy 2:12
d. 1 Peter 4:13–14
e. 1 Peter 5:10

d If we suffer because of our faith in Christ, when God's glory is revealed
we shall rejoice and be glad because we have glorified God.

c If we suffer with Christ, we shall also reign with Him.

a In this world we will have tribulation, but we can be encouraged
because Christ has overcome the world.

e After we have suffered, God has promised to perfect, strengthen,
establish, and settle us.

b Our present sufferings cannot be compared to God's glory, which will be revealed in us.

Personal Application

The existence of suffering and injustice is often a barrier that causes people to refuse to consider the love of God. However, suffering comes because people have free will and we live in a fallen world as a result of sin. In spite of our experience, believers have hope because:

- Christ died, so He understands our pain.
- Christ is risen, so we do not suffer alone.
- Christ will come again, so suffering and death will not prevail.

In light of God's grace, will you make a commitment to trust the Lord in spite of suffering, and encourage others to do the same? If so, write out your commitment in the space below.

Answers will vary.

4. Cross-Cultural Christianity

God is the Creator of all. He does not prefer one nationality over another because of class or skin color, nor does He prefer one individual over another because of their social position or material possessions.

Review the following verses. Then describe the hope that these truths provide for men and women of every race and culture.

a. Deuteronomy 10:17; 2 Chronicles 19:7
God is fearsome and mighty; He judges without partiality and cannot be bribed.

b. Acts 10:34–35, 43
God is no respecter of persons; He accepts people from every nation that fear Him, work righteously, and are declared righteous through Jesus Christ.

c. Romans 10:13
Anyone who calls on the name of the Lord will be saved.

d. Romans 12:11
There is no respect of persons with God.

e. Colossians 3:25
Anyone who does wrong will be judged by God.

Personal Application

How does the truth that God is no respecter of persons inspire you to embrace your culture as you worship and serve Him?

> Answers will vary.

How can this truth motivate you to transcend your culture and reach out to those who are different?

> Answers will vary.

Going Global

Dr. Martin Luther King Jr. combined the Exodus paradigm of God's liberation with the method of nonviolence and the message of love and hope found in the resurrection of Jesus Christ. Dr. King's hope in Christ sustained him in the midst of danger, grief, disappointment, and even in the face of death.

Read Romans 8:35–39. Describe how this same hope can sustain you, no matter what you may face today.

> Answers will vary.

Read 2 Corinthians 1:3–4. Describe how you can use this hope to encourage and strengthen others.

> The God of all comfort, who comforts us in our tribulation, enables us to comfort others with the same comfort that we have received from Him.

Chapter 3

Mission in the Motherland

Format for Sessions of 90 Minutes or More

PART ONE

MIN.	ACTIVITY
5	Prayer
10	Going Global Discussion
15	Introduction
20	Chapter Review
20	Life Application Discussion

PART TWO

MIN.	ACTIVITY
20	Small Group Study
15	Small Group Presentations
5	Large Group Presentations
5	Going Global Commitment
5	Going Global Commitment
5	Prayer

For sessions of less than 90 minutes, use PART ONE only and assign the Bible Application exercises as homework. Read the Going Global exercise at the end of the study aloud, and encourage the participants to come prepared to share their results next week. Then close the class in prayer.

*To complete the group study in PART TWO, each participant will need a copy of the student workbook that accompanies the book, *Going Global—Beyond the Boundaries.*

Lesson Aim: At the end of this two-part session, the participants should: (a) understand that African Americans have a rich heritage in the Bible; (b) identify God's motivation and goal for missions; (c) recognize early African American missionary efforts in Africa; (d) explain why African Americans should be concerned about missions to Africa; and (e) commit to review current events in Africa and pray of the needs of the people.

Key Verse: "Then Philip began with that very passage of Scripture and told him the good news about Jesus" (Acts 8:35, NIV).

Lesson Focus: African American missionaries were among the first to leave this country to share the Gospel. We sent the first African American missionaries to Africa in 1792. These African American missionaries risked being sold back into bondage in order to stand for justice and the Gospel of Jesus Christ.

Today we must rediscover the foundation they laid and build upon their legacy. We must become ready to boldly act upon the truth of God's Word. We must be willing to step out and declare justice, show mercy, and share the Good News of the Gospel of Jesus Christ.

PART ONE
Prayer

Open the session with prayer, including the lesson aim.

Going Global Discussion

Invite the participants to share the testimonies related to the Going Global exercise from last week's Bible study.

Introduction

Ask the participants to read the Key Verse aloud in unison. This verse appears at the beginning of chapter 3 in their workbooks. Then ask them to silently read the focus statement that follows this verse. If there are participants who do not have workbooks, read this statement aloud to the group.

Chapter Review

Use the following topics to review and discuss chapter 3.

- Africans in the Bible
- Early African American Missions Movement
- Current Missions in Africa

You may write these topics on the chalkboard or newsprint, or uncover them one at a time using an overhead projector and transparencies. Try to limit the discussion to five minutes or less for each topic.

Words You Should Know

It is often useful to define the terms that are discussed to ensure that the group shares a common understanding. Read or display the following definitions and allow a few minutes for questions or comments.

> • **Missions**—Sending someone forth to preach the Gospel in a culture or context that is different from their own; persons sent to a foreign land to share their faith or provide educational, medical, and other assistance.

- **Colonialism**—A system in which another country, territory, or political group takes over land and people outside its own boundaries, often to assume economic control over their resources, labor, and trade markets. The term also refers to the set of beliefs that legitimize and promote this exploitative system, especially the belief that the culture and customs of the colonizer are superior to those of the colonized.

- **Reconstruction**—The period of U.S. history after the American Civil War (1865–1877) when the southern states were reintegrated into the Union. To protect the civil rights of freed slaves, Congress enacted a Civil Rights Act in 1866 (and again in 1875). In addition, three constitutional amendments were passed: the Thirteenth, which abolished slavery; the Fourteenth, which granted civil rights to African Americans; and the Fifteenth, which granted the right to vote. However, these laws were ignored, and the South was allowed to establish a racist, segregated society. Almost 100 years later, the federal government was forced to address the illegal system of discrimination that was entrenched in the South by passing the Civil Rights Act of 1964.

Life Application Questions

Ask the participants to review and share their answers to the following Life Application questions:

- What steps can African American churches take to acknowledge our African heritage?
- Why should African American Christians share a unique burden for the unsaved in Africa?
- What African missions organizations do you know of and/or support?

These Life Application questions also appear in the student workbook with space to record their answers. You can ask the participants to take a few minutes to answer these questions. Or you can read the questions aloud or display them to facilitate discussion. You may also wish to share your point of view as a fellow participant in Bible study.

PART TWO
Small Group Study

Separating Small Groups. Ask the participants to form five small groups. Each group will study a different set of questions and report their findings to the larger group at the end of the study period.

Assign the Bible Application exercises as follows:

Group #1	Africans in the Bible
Group #2	The Motivation for Missions
Group #3	The Scope of Missions
Group #4	The Goal of Missions
Group #5	The Call to Missions

Feel free to tailor the small group study to fit the size and needs of your class. If your study group is small, you may focus on Bible Application exercises #1 and #5.

Set a Time Limit. About 15–20 minutes should be sufficient. Check the clock to determine how much time is available. Then notify the groups of the time that they should reconvene.

Sharing Insights. Encourage the small group members to vary their study methods. For example, the participants could locate different verses and take turns reading them aloud to the group. Then they could spend a few minutes discussing the answers to the questions. Or the group could divide the time in half. During the first part they each could read and answer all of the assigned questions. Then they would come together to discuss their answers and share insights and opinions. Remind them to include a discussion of the Personal Application questions as part of their study.

Preparing Reports. Have each small group select the participant(s) who will take notes, summarize the discussion, and present the group's findings.

Large Group Discussion

Reconvene the Group. Call the small groups back together.

Present Small Group Reports. Have the selected participants report the results of their small group study. Encourage the other groups to take notes, and allow time for discussion and questions within the larger group.

Monitor the Time. Remind the representatives to try to summarize the small group's discussion in two or three minutes. Allocate up to three minutes to discuss each group's presentation.

Going Global Commitment

Read the Going Global exercise aloud to the group. Then give the participants a few minutes to answer the question and make a personal commitment. Encourage them to come prepared to share what they have learned next week.

Closing

Ask the participants to read chapter 4 of *Going Global—Beyond the Boundaries* and record their notes at the end of their student workbooks. Remind them to bring their Bibles and workbooks to the next session. Close the class with prayer focused on the lesson aim.

Bible Application Exercises and Answers
1. Africans in the Bible

Due to the dominance of Western (White) culture, the presence of Africans in the Bible has been largely ignored or discounted. However, African Americans have a rich heritage in the Bible. Some of the African nations identified in the Bible are Egypt, Ethiopia (*Heb.*, Cush), and Libya (*Heb.*, Phut).

Match the following verses with the African person who is mentioned in the biblical passage.

> a. Genesis 9:18, 21; 10:6
> b. Genesis 16:1–4
> c. Exodus 2:21
> d. Jeremiah 38:7–11
> e. Matthew 27:32
> f. Acts 8:26–38
> g. Acts 13:1

c Zipporah, an Ethiopian, was the wife of Moses.

e Simon of Cyrene, a city in Libya (northern Africa), carried Jesus' cross.

d Ebed-Melech, an Ethiopian eunuch, saved the prophet Jeremiah.

a Ham, son of Noah, was the progenitor of African peoples.

f The Ethiopian eunuch asked Philip to explain the Scriptures; he believed, and was baptized.

g Simeon called Niger and Lucius of Cyrene were leaders in the church at Antioch.

b Hagar, an Egyptian, bore Abraham's first son.

Personal Application

The study of African and African American history is too vast and valuable to be relegated to a single month of the year, and it is too important to be taught solely by people who have a different cultural perspective. What steps can you take to discover and explore your own rich heritage? How will you share the information that you learn with others?

Answers will vary.

2. The Motivation for Missions

All Christian missionary efforts begin with God. The Bible clearly teaches that God is a "sending" God. In spite of our rebellion and sin, God has sent His messengers, His prophets, and finally His own Son to bring salvation to us.

Record the verses below as reminders of why God sent Jesus Christ.

a. John 3:17

"For God did not send his Son into the world to condemn the world, but to save the world through him."

b. Galatians 4:4–7

"But when the time had fully come, God sent his Son, born of a woman, born under law, to redeem those under law, that we might receive the full rights of sons. Because you are sons, God sent the Spirit of his Son into our hearts, the Spirit who calls out, 'Abba, Father.' So you are no longer a slave, but a son; and since you are a son, God has made you also an heir."

c. Ephesians 2:17–18

"He came and preached peace to you who were far away and peace to those who were near. For through him we both have access to the Father by one Spirit."

d. 1 John 4:9–10

"This is how God showed his love among us: He sent his one and only Son into the world that we might live through him. This is love: not that we loved God, but that he loved us and sent his Son as an atoning sacrifice for our sins."

Fill in the blanks for each statement below to describe our motivation for Christian missions.

a. Missionary efforts were demonstrated in the **work** of the Son (John 17:4).

b. Missionary efforts are made effective through the **power** of the Holy Spirit (Acts 1:8).

c. Missionary efforts spring from the **love** of the Father (1 John 3:1).

3. The Scope of Missions

God cares about every area of our lives. When Christ came, He not only preached the Good News, but He also cared for the poor, the needy, and the oppressed. Thus the Gospel is Good News that is expressed not only in words, but also in loving action and Christian service.

Read the verses below, and then summarize what they imply about the scope of Christian missions.

a. Luke 24:19

Jesus spoke and acted in authority and power before God and all the people.

b. Acts 10:38

God anointed Jesus with the Holy Ghost and with power, and Jesus went about doing good and healing all that were oppressed of the devil, for God was with Him.

c. Colossians 3:17

Whatever we do in word or deed, we should do in the name of our Lord Jesus and give thanks to God.

d. James 2:14–18

Faith not accompanied by practical actions that demonstrate God's love is not true Christian faith.

e. 1 John 3:18

We cannot just say that we love others; our actions must also reveal this truth.

4. The Goal of Missions

Just as missionary efforts begin with God, they also end with Him. Our mission is not to propagate a church, promote a religion, or reproduce our own point of view. The goal of missions is not a man-made agenda; it is the will and work of God.

Fill in the blanks below to identify God's role in missions.

      a. Without the Lord, we can do **nothing** (John 15:5).

      b. It is God who causes men and women to **believe** (Acts 11:21).

      c. Our **competence** for the task of missions comes from God (2 Corinthians 3:5).

      d. God **works** in and through us to do that which pleases Him (Philippians 2:13).

      f. God has **saved** us, and **called** us, not according to our works, but according to his own **purpose** and **grace,** which was given in Christ before the world began (2 Timothy 1:8–9).

Personal Application

In light of the differences between Christianity and "Christianity-ism," why is it important that the missionary efforts of the church reflect God's mission?

      Answers will vary.

5. The Call to Missions

Jesus was a missionary. He lived among the people, teaching the truth and showing the compassion of God. Following in His steps, we must also go into the world preaching the Gospel, teaching God's Word, and showing God's love and compassion to others.

Describe the mission that Jesus gave to His disciples (Matthew 10:7–8; Luke 9:2).

      Jesus sent the disciples forth to preach the Good News, heal the sick, and bring deliverance from sin and the power of the devil.

Describe what occurred when the disciples went out in obedience to the Lord's command (Mark 6:12–13; Luke 9:6).

      They departed and preached the Gospel and the need for repentance; they cast out devils and healed the sick everywhere.

Who was working with the disciples on their mission (Mark 16:20)?
The Lord was working with them.

Personal Application
Why is it important that we, who have received God's Good News, go out and tell it to others (Matthew 10:8; Romans 8:32)?
Answers will vary.

Going Global
God has called us to witness to people both near and far (cf. Acts 1:8). Because of our history and our heritage, African Americans should have a special interest in African missions.

List some ways that you and your church can increase your level of participation in missions to the Motherland.
Answers will vary.

Study current events in Africa, especially in places like Liberia, Rwanda, Burundi, and Sudan. Select particular needs and situations, like:

- Slaughter in Sudan
- Genocide in Rwanda
- Tribal wars in Burundi
- Spread of AIDS in sub-Saharan Africa
- Strongholds of Islam in Northern Africa
- Pervasiveness of poverty—the world's poorest nations are con centrated in Africa

Commit yourself to pray that the work and will of God will be done in these countries. Pray also for those that God sends to minister to the people.

Chapter 4

Empowerment and the North

Format for Sessions of 90 Minutes or More

PART ONE		PART TWO	
MIN.	ACTIVITY	MIN.	ACTIVITY
5	Prayer	20	Small Group Study
5	Going Global Discussion	15	Small Group Presentations
5	Introduction	15	Large Group Presentations
20	Chapter Review	5	Going Global Commitment
20	Life Application Discussion	5	Prayer

For sessions of less than 90 minutes, use PART ONE only and assign the Bible Application exercises as homework. Read the Going Global exercise at the end of the study aloud, and encourage the participants to come prepared to share their results next week. Then close the class in prayer.

*To complete the group study in PART TWO, each participant will need a copy of the student workbook that accompanies the book, *Going Global—Beyond the Boundaries.*

Lesson Aim: At the end of this two-part session, the participants should: (a) explain why it is important to view the events and situations of life from God's perspective; (b) describe how the quest for identity, dignity, and economic opportunity impacted the African American church during the 1900s; (c) understand how negative events can become an opportunity to witness; and (d) make a commitment to rely upon God's power for boldness to witness for Christ.

Key Verse: "They replied, 'Believe in the Lord Jesus, and you will be saved—you and your household'" (Acts 16:31, NIV).

Lesson Focus: Our African American identity, history, and culture is valued by God. It is time to correct the miseducation and lack of self-esteem that has caused our shame. It is time to discover the power of God at work in our lives to rescue, restore, empower, and equip us for our God-given purpose. The Gospel of Jesus Christ is the power of God unto salvation for everyone who believes. Let's not be ashamed to share this Good News with others.

PART ONE
Prayer

Open the session with prayer, including the lesson aim.

Going Global Discussion

Invite the participants to share what they learned as they completed their Going Global commitment from last week's Bible study.

Introduction

Ask the participants to read the Key Verse aloud in unison. This verse appears at the beginning of chapter 4 in their workbooks. Then ask them to silently read the focus statement that follows this verse. If there are participants who do not have workbooks, read this statement aloud to the group.

Chapter Review

Use the following topics to review and discuss chapter 4.

- The Quest for Opportunity and Empowerment
- African Identity and the African American Experience
- The African American Self-help Movement
- Marginalization and Institutional Racism

You may write these topics on the chalkboard or newsprint, or uncover them one at a time using an overhead projector and transparencies. Try to limit the discussion to five minutes or less for each topic.

Words You Should Know

It is often useful to define the terms that are discussed to ensure that the group shares a common understanding. Read or display the following definitions and allow a few minutes for questions or comments.

- **Institutional racism**—Prejudice and discrimination that is embedded in the structure and operation of corporate America and the society.
- **The Great Migration**—In the early 1900s, thousands of African Americans moved from the South to the North in search of greater economic, political, and social freedom.
- **Exile**—Removal from one's native land.
- **Judah paradigm**—The Old Testament record of the exile and captivity of the people of Judah and their restoration to their homeland.
- **Theology of empowerment**—The understanding that, like the people of Judah, African Americans were exiled from their homeland and the sense of identity and significance that accompanied the demand for civil rights and quest for equal opportunity.

Life Application Questions

Ask the participants to review and share their answers to the following Life Application questions:

- Describe the pattern of social gains and losses that African Americans have experienced.
- How can we guard against the continuation of this pattern in the future?
- How did the church serve as a place of empowerment during our struggle for civil rights?
- How can the church help to combat the institutional racism that continues to exist in America today?

These Life Application questions also appear in the student workbook with space to record their answers. You can ask the participants to take a few minutes to answer these questions. Or you can read the questions aloud or display them to facilitate discussion. You may also wish to share your point of view as a fellow participant in Bible study.

PART TWO
Small Group Study

Separating Small Groups. Ask the participants to form four small groups. Each group will study a different set of questions and report their findings to the larger group at the end of the study period. Assign the Bible Application exercises as follows:

Group #1   An Old Testament Pattern of Restoration
Group #2   The New Testament View of Redemption
Group #3   Viewing Events from God's Perspective
Group #4   Empowered by God

Feel free to tailor the small group study to fit the size and needs of your class. If your study group is small, you may focus on Bible Application exercises #3 and #4.

Set a Time Limit. About 15–20 minutes should be sufficient. Check the clock to determine how much time is available. Then notify the groups of the time that they should reconvene.

Sharing Insights. Encourage the small group members to vary their study methods. For example, the participants could locate different verses and take turns reading them aloud to the group. Then they could spend a few minutes discussing the answers to the questions. Or the group could divide the time in half. During the first part they each could read and answer all of the assigned questions. Then they would come together to discuss their answers and share insights and opinions. Remind them to include a discussion of the Personal Application questions as part of their study.

Preparing Reports. Have each small group select the participant(s) who will take notes, summarize the discussion, and present the group's findings.

Large Group Discussion
Reconvene the Group. Call the small groups back together.

Present Small Group Reports. Have the selected participants report the results of their small group study. Encourage the other groups to take notes, and allow time for discussion and questions within the larger group.

Monitor the Time. Remind the representatives to try to summarize the small group's discussion in two or three minutes. Allocate up to three minutes to discuss each group's presentation.

Going Global Commitment

Read the Going Global exercise aloud to the group. Then ask the participants if they are willing to step out to witness this week. If they agree, encourage them to share their adventures with the class next week.

Closing

Ask the participants to read chapter 5 of *Going Global—Beyond the Boundaries* and record their notes at the end of their student workbooks. Remind them to bring their Bibles and workbooks to the next session. Close the class with prayer focused on the lesson aim.

Bible Application Exercises and Answers

1. An Old Testament Pattern of Restoration

The theology of empowerment was based on the Old Testament paradigm of Judah's exile and restoration. This served to motivate many African Americans to travel North in search of employment and fair treatment.

Read 2 Chronicles 36:15–21. Then use the space below to briefly summarize the story of Judah's exile in your own words.

> Answers will vary. The passage describes how, at the end of the 70-year period, the people of Judah were restored to their homeland, where they rebuilt the walls of Jerusalem and the temple of God.

Leviticus 25:9–17 describes the year of Jubilee. Read this passage. Then use verse 10 to write down what was proclaimed and what was returned.

> Liberty, or freedom, was proclaimed to all the inhabitants. Each person's possessions were returned, and people returned to their families.

Personal Application

The American Industrial Revolution produced a profusion of jobs and the popular "melting pot" concept promised acceptance and fair treatment. However, many African Americans who hoped for restoration and freedom in the "land of opportunity" failed to find it. As God was abandoned, the search for empowerment became the Black Power Movement and the fight for equality changed.

In your opinion, what could the church have done to prevent the "theological vacuum" during this period?

> Answers will vary.

When others face situations of injustice, unfairness, disappointment, or pain, what things can you do to help? How can you encourage them to seek the Lord?

> Answers will vary.

2. The New Testament View of Redemption

The disciples initially expected the Messiah to establish an earthly kingdom. However, Jesus came to establish the reign of God in the hearts of men and women, and to restore our intimate relationship with Him. We look forward to the day when "the kingdoms of this earth have become the kingdom of our God."

Record what the following verses teach us about our redemption in Christ.

    a. Romans 3:23–24

> We have been justified by God's grace.

    b. Titus 2:14

> We have been redeemed, purchased, and purified to become God's people, who are fervently doing good works.

    c. Ephesians 1:7; 1 Peter 1:18–19

> We have been redeemed by the blood of the Lamb.

Record what the following verses reveal about some of the rewards of our redemption.

a. Matthew 6:20

> We have treasures in heaven.

b. John 14:2–3; 2 Corinthians 5:1

> We have a prepared and prosperous place in the Father's house.

c. Romans 8:11; Galatians 4:7

> We are heirs of God and joint-heirs with Christ.

d. James 1:12; Revelation 2:10

> We will receive the crown of life.

Personal Application

Every believer in Christ has been redeemed. You were "bought with a price: therefore glorify God in your body, and in your spirit, which are God's" (1 Corinthians 6:20, KJV). Decide what you will do to honor God with your body and with your spirit. List your commitments below.

> Answers will vary.

3. Viewing Events from God's Perspective

God's ways and thoughts are much higher than ours. Therefore, if we desire to do His will, we cannot rely on our own limited understanding.

Review the following verses and identify how these men and women viewed their situations through the lens of their faith in God. Then describe how their faith shaped their response to the challenges they faced.

a. Abraham—Genesis 22:1–8

> Abraham was obedient to God, and he had faith that God would provide a lamb.

b. Joseph—Genesis 45:4–8; 50:20

> Joseph told his brothers that although they had sold him as a slave, God turned the situation around and made him a ruler in Egypt in order to save others.

c. Joshua and Caleb—Numbers 13:30; 14:30–38

> Joshua and Caleb had the faith to believe that they were able to overcome the giants and take the land that God had given to the Israelites.

d. David—1 Samuel 17:34-37

David declared that the Lord, who had given him the strength to kill the lion and the bear, would enable him to slay the giant that dared to defy the armies of the living God.

e. The Shunammite woman—2 Kings 4:17-36

She believed that the prophet would be able to revive her dead son. She refused to stop until she reached him with her desperate plea for help.

f. Shadrach, Meshach, and Abednego—Daniel 3:13-18

They refused to serve false gods or worship an idol even if it cost their lives. They stood before the king and proclaimed God's power and deliverance and their faith in Him.

g. Mary—Luke 1:34-38

She believed the angel's report that she would conceive the Son of God.

h. Paul and Silas—Acts 16:22-26

After being beaten and imprisoned unjustly, they prayed and sang praises to God and were freed by an earthquake.

Personal Application

Has there ever been a time when the Word of God changed your view of a situation or challenge that you were facing? Have you ever been in a situation when your faith in God sustained you? Has there been a time when prayer made the difference?

Briefly describe a few of these situations below. Keep a record of the times that God has shown up in your life so that you will be ready to use your testimony to encourage someone else.

Answers will vary.

4. Empowered by God

God has given us the power to do His will.

Match the following verses with the power that believers possess.

a. Matthew 16:19; 18:18

b. Matthew 18:19; Luke 11:9

c. Matthew 18:20; Luke 11:9
d. Ephesians 3:20; 6:10

d Spiritual power

a Spiritual authority

c Divine presence

b Answered prayer

Record and memorize the following verses. Use them as reminders of your power source.

a. Zechariah 4:6b
"'Not by might nor by power, but by my Spirit,' says the LORD Almighty."

b. 2 Corinthians 3:5
"Not that we are competent in ourselves to claim anything for ourselves, but our competence comes from God."

c. 2 Corinthians 4:7
"But we have this treasure in jars of clay to show that this all-surpassing power is from God and not from us."

Going Global

Second Corinthians 5:7 says, "We live by faith, not by sight." Be willing to step out. Let this truth spur you to go forth in the power of God and become a bold witness for Christ.

Chapter 5

Early African American Theologians

Format for Sessions of 90 Minutes or More

PART ONE		PART TWO	
MIN.	ACTIVITY	MIN.	ACTIVITY
5	Prayer	20	Small Group Study
5	Going Global Discussion	15	Small Group Presentations
5	Introduction	15	Large Group Presentations
15	Chapter Review	5	Going Global Commitment
20	Life Application Discussion	5	Prayer

For sessions of less than 90 minutes, use PART ONE only and assign the Bible Application exercises as homework. Read the Going Global exercise at the end of the study aloud, and encourage the participants to come prepared to share their results next week. Then close the class in prayer.

*To complete the group study in PART TWO, each participant will need a copy of the student workbook that accompanies the book, *Going Global—Beyond the Boundaries.*

Lesson Aim: At the end of this two-part session, the participants should: (a) know that African Americans have a rich church history; (b) recognize that the early African American theologians were committed to freedom and involved in missions to Africa; (c) realize that, as Jesus' followers, we have been commissioned and empowered to take the Gospel to others; and (d) identify some practical ways to share the truth and freedom that is available through Jesus Christ.

Key Verse: "Therefore go and make disciples of all nations, baptizing them in the name of the Father and of the Son and of the Holy Spirit, and teaching them to obey everything I have commanded you. And surely I am with you always, to the very end of the age" (Matthew 28:19–20, NIV).

Lesson Focus: African American theologians have historically emphasized missions and ministry. Because of our life experiences, Black theology must go beyond an academic understanding of God and arguments about His nature or existence. It must be relevant and address real-world issues as it reveals who God is, what God has done in the past, and what He can do to change the problems we face today.

PART ONE
Prayer

Open the session with prayer, including the lesson aim.

Going Global Discussion

Invite the participants to share the results of their Going Global commitment to witness from last week's Bible study.

Introduction

Ask the participants to read the Key Verse aloud in unison. This verse appears at the beginning of chapter 5 in their workbooks. Then ask them to silently read the focus statement that follows this verse. If there are participants who do not have workbooks, read this statement aloud to the group.

Chapter Review

Use the following topics to review and discuss chapter 5.

- Early African American Theologians
- How They Applied God's Word in Their Situations

You may write these topics on the chalkboard or newsprint, or uncover them one at a time using an overhead projector and transparencies. Try to limit the discussion to five minutes or less for each topic.

Words You Should Know

It is often useful to define the terms that are discussed to ensure that the group shares a common understanding. Read or display the following definitions and allow a few minutes for questions or comments.

- **Antebellum**—The pre-Civil War period in the United States where the practice of slavery, racism, and other abuses of human rights were part of life in the Old South.

- **Diaspora**—A group of people or ethnic population forced to leave their homeland and scattered throughout other parts of the world, and the subsequent developments in their dispersal and culture.

- **African Diaspora**—The movement of Africans taken into slavery and the dispersion of their culture and descendants throughout the world.

Life Application Questions

Ask the participants to review and share their answers to the following Life Application questions:

- African Americans have a rich church history. How many African American theologians are you familiar with?
- Do you know the history of your denomination?
- Do you know your local church history?
- What sources can you use to gain additional knowledge in these important areas?

These Life Application questions also appear in the student workbook with space to record their answers. You can ask the participants to take a few minutes to answer these questions. Or you can read the questions aloud or display them to facilitate discussion. You may also wish to share your point of view as a fellow participant in Bible study.

PART TWO
Small Group Study

Separating Small Groups. Ask the participants to form three small groups. Each group will study a different set of questions and report their findings to the larger group at the end of the study period. Assign the Bible Application exercises as follows:

Group #1   Remembering the Past
Group #2   What Believers Should Remember
Group #3   African American Theologians

Feel free to tailor the small group study to fit the size and needs of your class. If your study group is small, you may focus on Bible Application exercise #3.

Set a Time Limit. About 15–20 minutes should be sufficient. Check the clock to determine how much time is available. Then notify the groups of the time that they should reconvene.

Sharing Insights. Encourage the small group members to vary their study methods. For example, the participants could locate different verses and take turns reading them aloud to the group. Then they could spend a few minutes discussing the answers to the questions. Or the group could divide the time in half. During the first part they each could read and answer all of the assigned questions. Then they would come together to discuss their answers and share insights and opinions. Remind them to include a discussion of the Personal Application questions as part of their study.

Preparing Reports. Have each small group select the participant(s) who will take notes, summarize the discussion, and present the group's findings.

Large Group Discussion
Reconvene the Group. Call the small groups back together.

Present Small Group Reports. Have the selected participants report the results of their small group study. Encourage the other groups to take notes, and allow time for discussion and questions within the larger group.

Monitor the Time. Remind the representatives to try to summarize the small group's discussion in two or three minutes. Allocate up to three minutes to discuss each group's presentation.

Going Global Commitment
Read the Going Global exercise aloud to the group. Then give the participants a few minutes to answer the question and encourage them to share their suggestions next week.

Closing
Ask the participants to read chapter 6 of *Going Global—Beyond the Boundaries* and record their notes at the end of their student workbooks. Remind them to bring their Bibles and workbooks to the next session. Close the class with prayer focused on the lesson aim.

Bible Application Exercises and Answers
1. Remembering the Past
History is important. In fact, the Bible itself is a record of God's acts throughout history. The Bible also contains numerous examples of God's instructions to remember the past. As believers, it is not enough to look

back at our history and remember our experiences. We must view those experiences in light of God's Word. The Lord stands above history to point us to destiny.

In Joshua 4:1–7, 20–24, Joshua set up stones of remembrance. Review this passage and use it to answer the following questions.

> a. Who gave the instruction (v. 1)?
> The Lord

> b. Who obeyed the instruction (v. 4)?
> Joshua

> c. Why was the instruction given? (v. 6)?
> To serve as a sign among the people and a testimony to their children

> d. What did the Lord want them to remember (vv. 23–24)?
> How God has miraculously acted on their behalf to dry up the Jordan so they could cross on dry ground

> e. Why did the Lord want them to remember (v. 24)?
> So that all the people would fear the Lord and know that He is powerful

In 1 Corinthians 10:1–6, 11, Paul used the Israelites' past to warn believers. Review this passage and use it to answer the following questions.

> a. What events were they told to remember (vv. 1–5)?
> How the Israelites had been led by a cloud, crossed the Jordan, ate manna in the wilderness, and drank from the rock that represented Christ, yet many doubted and disobeyed God and died in the wilderness

> b. Why are they told to remember these things (vv. 6, 11)?
> So that they would not make the same mistakes but instead would learn from their example

Personal Application
List some past events that you feel African Americans should be careful to remember. Explain why.
> Answers will vary.

List some lessons that we can learn from the past that could serve as warnings in the future.
>Answers will vary.

2. What Believers Should Remember

The Lord has done great things for us. Therefore, it is important that we never forget His demonstrated grace and love.

Look up Luke 22:19 and 1 Corinthians 11:24–25 to identify the event that believers are told to remember in the New Testament.
>We are told to remember Jesus' death on the Cross for us.

Use the following verses to identify some other things that believers are instructed to remember.

>a. Psalm 103:2–5
>>Remember the blessings and benefits that the Lord has provided for us.

>b. Psalm 143:5
>>Remember the old days and mediate on the works of the Lord.

>c. Ecclesiastes 12:1
>>Remember the Creator in the days of your youth.

>d. Ephesians 2:11–13
>>Remember that we have been forgiven of our sins and reconciled to God through Jesus Christ.

>e. Colossians 3:16
>>Remember God's Word.

Review John 14:26 and describe how the Holy Spirit helps us.
>The Holy Spirit teaches us and reminds us of God's Word.

Personal Application

Why is it important for believers of every race and culture to remember their Christian heritage?
>Answers will vary.

Think about the faith of our forebears, who believed in God despite the brutality of slavery, racism, and injustice. How can reminders of their faith help us to face the future?

Answers will vary.

3. African American Theologians

The early African American theologians applied God's Word in their situations and took action based on their faith.

Write the following verses. Then explain how these truths can be used to correct attitudes of prejudice or racism among believers.

a. Acts 10:34

"Then Peter began to speak: 'I now realize how true it is that God does not show favoritism.'"

b. Acts 17:26–27

"From one man he made every nation of men, that they should inhabit the whole earth; and he determined the times set for them and the exact places where they should live. God did this so that men would seek him and per-haps reach out for him and find him, though he is not far from each of us."

c. 1 Corinthians 12:13

"For we were all baptized by one Spirit into one body—whether Jews or Greeks, slave or free—and we were all given the one Spirit to drink."

d. Galatians 3:28

"There is neither Jew nor Greek, slave nor free, male nor female, for you are all one in Christ Jesus."

e. Colossians 3:10–11

"And have put on the new self, which is being renewed in knowledge in the image of its Creator. Here there is no Greek or Jew, circumcised or uncircumcised, barbarian, Scythian, slave or free, but Christ is all, and is in all."

Read Genesis 28:16–19. Why do you think Richard Allen would select "Bethel" for the name of the church that he founded?

"Bethel" means the house of God; it was the name that Jacob

gave to the place where he had a vision of the angels of God ascending and descending on the ladder whose top reached unto heaven.

Read James 2:1–9. Why would Rev. James W. C. Pennington oppose the colonization of Africa?
God's Word teaches us to love our neighbors and not to disrespect others because of their lack of power or position in this world.

Read James 4:7 and 1 Peter 5:8–9. Describe how these verses relate to Henry Highland Garnet's call for resistance.
Slavery was the evil that Garnet was calling African Americans to resist.

Read Luke 12:48. How does this verse relate to assertions by Lewis Woodson, Rev. Alexander Crummell, and others that African Americans have a special responsibility to help Africans?
Many African Americans are blessed by God both spiritually and physically; therefore, we should share what we have with others. Like Esther and Joseph, God may have sustained us through times of racism and slavery in order to use us to help those in our native land.

Going Global

"Then said Jesus to those Jews which believed on him, If ye continue in my word, then are ye my disciples indeed; And ye shall know the truth, and the truth shall make you free" (John 8:31–32, KJV).

Think of specific ways that you and your church can be used by God to bring truth and freedom to others around the world. Write your suggestions below.
Answers will vary.

Chapter 6

Applying Biblical Truth

Format for Sessions of 90 Minutes or More

PART ONE		PART TWO	
MIN.	ACTIVITY	MIN.	ACTIVITY
5	Prayer	20	Small Group Study
5	Going Global Discussion	15	Small Group Presentations
5	Introduction	15	Large Group Presentations
15	Chapter Review	5	Going Global Commitment
20	Life Application Discussion	5	Prayer

For sessions of less than 90 minutes, use PART ONE only and assign the Bible Application exercises as homework. Read the Going Global exercise at the end of the study aloud, and encourage the participants to come prepared to share their results next week. Then close the class in prayer.

*To complete the group study in PART TWO, each participant will need a copy of the student workbook that accompanies the book, *Going Global—Beyond the Boundaries.*

Lesson Aim: At the end of this two-part session, the participants should: (a) commit to study the Bible and apply its principles to the situations they face in life; and (b) commit to share the Gospel through evangelism and action.

Key Verse: "How beautiful on the mountains are the feet of those who bring good news, who proclaim peace, who bring good tidings, who proclaim salvation, who say to Zion, 'Your God reigns!'" (Isaiah 52:7, NIV).

Lesson Focus: The world of missions needs African American Christians. Black believers know instinctively and intuitively that God is concerned about every aspect of our existence and His compassion is active and powerful to effect change in lives of people around the world.

PART ONE
Prayer
Open the session with prayer, including the lesson aim.

Going Global Discussion
Invite the participants to share their suggestions from the Going Global exercise in last week's Bible study.

Introduction
Ask the participants to read the Key Verse aloud in unison. This verse appears at the beginning of chapter 6 in their workbooks. Then ask them to silently read the focus statement that follows this verse. If there are participants who do not have workbooks, read this statement aloud to the group.

Chapter Review
Use the following topics to review and discuss chapter 6.

- Developing a Theological Understanding
- Applying God's Word
- Seeking God's Perspective

You may write these topics on the chalkboard or newsprint, or uncover them one at a time using an overhead projector and transparencies. Try to limit the discussion to five minutes or less for each topic.

Words You Should Know
It is often useful to define the terms that are discussed to ensure that the group shares a common understanding. Read or display the following definitions and allow a few minutes for questions or comments.

- **Praxis**—The exercise or practice of an art, science, or skill; putting biblical truth into action.

- **Biblical paradigm**—The identification a basic biblical pattern that connects with our current situation.

Life Application Questions
Ask the participants to review and share their answers to the following Life Application questions:

- Why should we apply the Word of God to every area of life?

• Since God doesn't think like us, how do we develop His perspective?

These Life Application questions also appear in the student workbook with space to record their answers. You can ask the participants to take a few minutes to answer these questions. Or you can read the questions aloud or display them to facilitate discussion. You may also wish to share your point of view as a fellow participant in Bible study.

PART TWO
Small Group Study

Separating Small Groups. Ask the participants to form two groups. Each group will study a different set of questions and report their findings to the larger group at the end of the study period.

Assign the Bible Application exercises as follows:

Group #1   Understanding Biblical Truth
Group #2   Discovering Biblical Principles

Feel free to tailor the small group study to fit the size and needs of your class. If your study group is small, you may focus on Bible Application exercise #2.

Set a Time Limit. About 15–20 minutes should be sufficient. Check the clock to determine how much time is available. Then notify the groups of the time that they should reconvene.

Sharing Insights. Encourage the small group members to vary their study methods. For example, the participants could locate different verses and take turns reading them aloud to the group. Then they could spend a few minutes discussing the answers to the questions. Or the group could divide the time in half. During the first part they each could read and answer all of the assigned questions. Then they would come together to discuss their answers and share insights and opinions. Remind them to include a discussion of the Personal Application questions as part of their study.

Preparing Reports. Have each small group select the participant(s) who will take notes, summarize the discussion, and present the group's findings.

Large Group Discussion

Reconvene the Group. Call the small groups back together.

Present Small Group Reports. Have the selected participants report the results of their small group study. Encourage the other groups to take notes, and allow time for discussion and questions within the larger group.

Monitor the Time. Remind the representatives to try to summarize the small group's discussion in two or three minutes. Allocate up to three minutes to discuss each group's presentation.

Going Global Commitment

Read the Going Global exercise. Then give the participants a few minutes to answer the question and write a personal commitment statement. Encourage them to come prepared to share the results next week.

Closing

Ask the participants to read chapter 7 of *Going Global—Beyond the Boundaries* and record their notes at the end of their student workbooks. Remind them to bring their Bibles and workbooks to the next session. Close the class with prayer focused on the lesson aim.

Bible Application Exercises and Answers

1. Understanding Biblical Truth

Before we can apply or act on biblical truth, we must first recognize and understand it. As we study God's Word, pray for understanding, and apply it to our situation, we will grow spiritually and glorify God.

Read Psalm 119. Then use it to list some of the things that we should do to develop our understanding of God's Word.

Answers will vary. They could include the following:

respect it (v. 6)
memorize it (v. 11)
declare it (v. 13)
meditate on it (v. 15)
delight in it (v. 16)
understand it (v. 27)
draw strength from it (v. 28)
obey it whole-heartedly (v. 34)
hope in it (v. 74)
know it (v. 79)
remember it (v. 93)
seek it (v. 94)
consider it (v. 95)

enjoy it (v. 103)
rejoice in it (v. 111)
fear it (v. 120)
long for it (v. 131) ✔
love it (v. 140)
praise God for it (v. 164)
pray for understanding of it (v. 169)
choose it (v. 173)
do not forget it (v. 176)

Bible study is an important part of our spiritual life. Use the verses below to identify some of the ways that God's Word affects our lives.

a. John 17:17
It sanctifies us.

b. 2 Timothy 2:15
It causes us not to be ashamed.

c. 2 Timothy 3:16–17
It is profitable for teaching, rebuking, and correcting, and training in righteousness so that we might be prepared to do good works.

d. Hebrews 4:12
It discerns the thoughts and intentions of the heart.

e. 1 Peter 2:2
It causes us to grow spiritually.

Personal Application
What can you do to increase your understanding of God's Word?
Answers will vary.

2. Discovering Biblical Principles
As we examine basic biblical patterns and prayerfully match them with similar experiences in our lives, we can see biblical principles. As we discover these principles, we can begin to obey them.

Review Matthew 26:31–46. Use this passage to answer the following questions:

a. How was God in control of the situation then?
Answers will vary.
b. How was God speaking to the situation then?
Answers will vary.

c. How was God present in the situation then?
Answers will vary.

Now relate Matthew 26:31–46 to your work in missions. With this in mind, answer the following questions:

a. How is God in control of our situation now?
Answers will vary.

b. How is God speaking to our situation now?
Answers will vary.

c. How is God present in our situation now?
Answers will vary.

Review Luke 18:18–30. Use this passage to answer the following questions:

a. How was God in control of the situation then?
Answers will vary.

b. How was God speaking to the situation then?
Answers will vary.

c. How was God present in the situation then?
Answers will vary.

Now relate Luke 18:18–30 to your work in missions. With this in mind, answer the following questions:

a. How is God in control of our situation now?
Answers will vary.

b. How is God speaking to our situation now?
Answers will vary.

c. How is God present in our situation now?
Answers will vary.

Personal Application

Identify several practical ways that you can apply the principles from Matthew 26:31–46 in your missionary activities.

> Answers will vary.

Identify several practical ways that you can apply the principles from Luke 18:18–30 in your missionary activities.

> Answers will vary.

Going Global

Isaiah 52:7 (KJV) declares, "How beautiful upon the mountains are the feet of him that bringeth good tidings, that publisheth peace; that bringeth good tidings of good, that publisheth salvation; that saith unto Zion, Thy God reigneth!"

How are your feet? Are they "shod with the preparation of the gospel of peace" (Ephesians 6:15, KJV)? Will you make a commitment to go where God sends you and share the Gospel through your words and deeds this week? If so, write a statement of your commitment below.

> Answers will vary.

Chapter 7

Called to Righteousness— Transcending the Culture

Format for Sessions of 90 Minutes or More

PART ONE		PART TWO	
MIN.	ACTIVITY	MIN.	ACTIVITY
5	Prayer	20	Small Group Study
5	Going Global Discussion	15	Small Group Presentations
5	Introduction	15	Large Group Presentations
15	Chapter Review	5	Going Global Commitment
20	Life Application Discussion	5	Prayer

For sessions of less than 90 minutes, use PART ONE only and assign the Bible Application exercises as homework. Read the Going Global exercise at the end of the study aloud, and encourage the participants to come prepared to share their results next week. Then close the class in prayer.

*To complete the group study in PART TWO, each participant will need a copy of the student workbook that accompanies the book, *Going Global—Beyond the Boundaries.*

Lesson Aim: At the end of this two-part session, the participants should: (a) identify some ways that the African American church can biblically address today's issues and take a stand against unrighteousness, injustice, ungodliness, and oppression; (b) explain how believers can become agents of righteousness and proponents of justice in the world today; and (c) commit to seek righteousness and make a difference by becoming involved in a relief effort or organized political, social, or missionary action.

Key Verse: "Therefore, as we have opportunity, let us do good to all people, especially to those who belong to the family of believers" (Galatians 6:10, NIV).

Lesson Focus: The African American church has been a voice and source of strength for our people in the past. It has served as a place of refuge and a weapon against injustice and racism in America. As the battle continues, the church must stand against unrighteousness in all its forms. As we live to please the Lord, we are called to demonstrate righteousness that transcends the culture.

PART ONE
Prayer

Open the session with prayer, including the lesson aim.

Going Global Discussion

Invite the participants to share the results of their Going Global commitment from last week's Bible study.

Introduction

Ask the participants to read the Key Verse aloud in unison. This verse appears at the beginning of chapter 7 in their workbooks. Then ask them to silently read the focus statement that follows this verse. If there are participants who do not have workbooks, read this statement aloud to the group.

Chapter Review

Use the following topics to review and discuss chapter 7.

- Components of Unrighteousness
- Components of Righteousness
- Pursuing the Righteousness of God

You may write these topics on the chalkboard or newsprint, or uncover them one at a time using an overhead projector and transparencies. Try to limit the discussion to five minutes or less for each topic.

Words You Should Know

It is often useful to define the terms that are discussed to ensure that the group shares a common understanding. Read or display the following definitions and allow a few minutes for questions or comments.

- **Righteousness**—Holy and upright living in accordance with God's standard.

- **Unrighteousness**—The effect of sin and wrongdoing.

Life Application Questions

Ask the participants to review and share their answers to the following Life Application questions:

- How would you describe the African American culture today?
- How has our culture changed in the past 10–20 years?
- How has it remained the same?

These Life Application questions also appear in the student workbook with space to record their answers. You can ask the participants to take a few minutes to answer these questions. Or you can read the questions aloud or display them to facilitate discussion. You may also wish to share your point of view as a fellow participant in Bible study.

PART TWO
Small Group Study

Separating Small Groups. Ask the participants to form two groups. Each group will study a different set of questions and report their findings to the larger group at the end of the study period.

Assign the Bible Application exercises as follows:

Group #1   Demonstrating Righteousness
Group #2   Resisting Unrighteousness

Feel free to tailor the small group study to fit the size and needs of your class. If your study group is small, you may focus on Bible Application exercise #2.

Set a Time Limit. About 15–20 minutes should be sufficient. Check the clock to determine how much time is available. Then notify the groups of the time that they should reconvene.

Sharing Insights. Encourage the small group members to vary their study methods. For example, the participants could locate different verses and take turns reading them aloud to the group. Then they could spend a few minutes discussing the answers to the questions. Or the group could divide the time in half. During the first part they each could read and answer all of the assigned questions. Then they would come together to discuss their answers and share insights and opinions. Remind them to include a discussion of the Personal Application questions as part of their study.

Preparing Reports. Have each small group select the participant(s) who will take notes, summarize the discussion, and present the group's findings.

Large Group Discussion

Reconvene the Group. Call the small groups back together.

Present Small Group Reports. Have the selected participants report the results of their small group study. Encourage the other groups to take notes, and allow time for discussion and questions within the larger group.

Monitor the Time. Remind the representatives to try to summarize the small group's discussion in two or three minutes. Allocate up to three minutes to discuss each group's presentation.

Going Global Commitment

Read the Going Global exercise aloud to the group. Then give the participants a few minutes to answer the question. Encourage them to add other thoughts and possible actions to their list during the week. Remind them to be prepared to share some of their suggestions in class next week.

Closing

Ask the participants to read chapter 8 of *Going Global—Beyond the Boundaries* and record their notes at the end of their student workbooks. Remind them to bring their Bibles and workbooks to the next session. Close the class with prayer focused on the lesson aim.

Bible Application Exercises and Answers

1. Demonstrating Righteousness

As we look around, it is obvious that we live in an unjust world. However, as followers of Christ, we are called to live out our faith in a way that reveals the righteousness of God.

Use the following verses to review and record some things the Bible says about righteousness.

> a. Isaiah 64:6
>> Our human righteousness is like filthy rags in comparison to God's righteous standard.

b. Matthew 5:6

Those who sincerely long for the righteousness of God will be satisfied.

c. Matthew 6:33

Our highest priority in life should be to seek the kingdom of God and His righteousness.

d. Romans 3:22; Philippians 3:9

We obtain the righteousness of God through faith in Jesus Christ.

e. Romans 14:17

God's kingdom is righteousness, peace, and joy in the Holy Spirit.

f. 2 Corinthians 5:20

We have received righteousness through a great exchange. Our sinless Savior became sin for us so that we might be made righteous.

g. Ephesians 6:14

We are instructed to put on the breastplate of righteousness.

h. Titus 3:5–6

We are saved not because of our righteousness but because of God's mercy.

Use the following verses to identify some things the Bible says about justice.

a. Psalm 82:3

We should defend the weak and fatherless, and do justice to the poor and needy.

b. Proverbs 21:3

To do what is right is more acceptable to God than sacrifice.

c. Isaiah 9:6–7

The kingdom of God will be established with justice and righteousness.

Read the following verses and record some things the Bible says about godliness.

> a. I Timothy 3:16
>> The mystery of godliness is equated with the Gospel of Jesus Christ.
>
> b. I Timothy 4:8
>> Godliness is profitable both now in this life and in eternity.
>
> c. I Timothy 6:6
>> "Godliness with contentment is great gain."
>
> d. I Timothy 6:11
>> We should pursue godliness.

Personal Application

List three forms of unrighteousness that you are confronted by each day.
> Answers will vary.

List three areas of injustice that you feel are serious problems in this country today.
> Answers will vary.

2. Resisting Unrighteousness

It has been said that all that is necessary for evil to triumph is for good men to do nothing. As the body of Christ, we must work together to do God's will in this world.

Review the following verses to determine how believers can live godly lives in a sinful world.

> a. Romans 12:2
>> We should not conform to the way of the world; instead, we must transform our minds with the Word of God.
>
> b. Romans 12:21; I Peter 3:9
>> We should overcome evil with good.
>
> c. Titus 2:11–12
>> We should deny ungodliness and worldly lusts, and live soberly, righteously, and godly in this present world.

d. 1 John 1:9

    If we sin, we should confess and repent so that God might cleanse us from all unrighteousness.

e. 1 John 2:15

    Refuse to love the world and the things in the world.

f. Jude 20–23

    We should separate ourselves from the world, build our faith, pray in the Holy Spirit, keep ourselves in the love of God, have compassion, make a difference, and with fear rescue sinners by bring them to Christ for salvation.

What is the ultimate result of unrighteousness and injustice?

a. Romans 1:18

    God's wrath will be revealed.

b. Romans 2:8–9

    Wrath, anger, trouble, and distress will come upon every soul of those who do evil.

c. 2 Thessalonians 2:10

    Those who are unrighteous will perish.

Personal Application

In light of the cultural unrighteousness that surrounds us, identify two things that the church can do to address institutional racism and oppression.

    Answers will vary.

Are you presently involved in any organized activity or effort to combat human suffering or injustice? If so, list your involvement below. If not, list some ways that you can become more involved.

    Answers will vary.

Going Global

Great numbers of people lost their lives in recent tragedies, such as September 11th, the tsunami disaster, hurricanes, earthquakes, and ongoing armed conflicts around the world. Galatians 6:10 (KJV) teaches, "As we have therefore opportunity, let us do good unto all men, especially unto them who are of the household of faith."

Brainstorm some ways that your church can create new opportunities to "do good" in these situations where the need is great. List your suggestions below.

Answers will vary.

Chapter 8

Traditional Models of African American Churches

Format for Sessions of 90 Minutes or More

PART ONE		PART TWO	
MIN.	**ACTIVITY**	**MIN.**	**ACTIVITY**
5	Prayer	20	Small Group Study
5	Going Global Discussion	15	Small Group Presentations
5	Introduction	15	Large Group Presentations
15	Chapter Review	5	Going Global Commitment
20	Life Application Discussion	5	Prayer

For sessions of less than 90 minutes, use PART ONE only and assign the Bible Application exercises as homework. Read the Going Global exercise at the end of the study aloud, and encourage the participants to come prepared to share their results next week. Then close the class in prayer.

*To complete the group study in PART TWO, each participant will need a copy of the student workbook that accompanies the book, *Going Global—Beyond the Boundaries.*

Lesson Aim: At the end of this two-part session, the participants should: (a) describe the decline of missions activity in the African American church; (b) identify three models of traditional African American churches and describe why they were unable to transform the culture; and (c) recognize how we can communicate the Gospel to those who may feel they don't need the Savior.

Key Verse: "Jesus answered, 'I am the way and the truth and the life. No one comes to the Father except through me'" (John 14:6, NIV).

Lesson Focus: The traditional Black church served an important purpose. It was a place of hope and healing, a place where Black people found God and each other. It was a place of foot stomping and shouting, of spirituals and gospel songs, of prophetic preaching and social action.

However, the church cannot rely upon tradition. We must move forward to engage our culture with the unchanging Word of God.

PART ONE
Prayer
Open the session with prayer, including the lesson aim.

Going Global Discussion
Invite the participants to share their suggestions from the Going Global exercise in last week's Bible study.

Introduction
Ask the participants to read the Key Verse aloud in unison. This verse appears at the beginning of chapter 8 in their workbooks. Then ask them to silently read the focus statement that follows this verse. If there are participants who do not have workbooks, read this statement aloud to the group.

Chapter Review
Use the following topics to review and discuss chapter 8.

- African American Church History
- Models of the Traditional Church
- The Impact of the Church on the Culture

You may write these topics on the chalkboard or newsprint, or uncover them one at a time using an overhead projector and transparencies. Try to limit the discussion to five minutes or less for each topic.

Words You Should Know
It is often useful to define the terms that are discussed to ensure that the group shares a common understanding. Read or display the following definition and allow a few minutes for questions or comments.

- **The church**—This word carries several meanings. It can refer to the body of Christ, which is comprised of all Christian believers throughout the world; a religious denomination; a building made for public worship; a local group of believers who worship in a particular place; or an individual believer in Jesus Christ.

Life Application Questions

Ask the participants to review and share their answers to the following Life Application questions:

- What models or denominations of African American churches are you most familiar with?
- How would you describe them?

These Life Application questions also appear in the student workbook with space to record their answers. You can ask the participants to take a few minutes to answer these questions. Or you can read the questions aloud or display them to facilitate discussion. You may also wish to share your point of view as a fellow participant in Bible study.

PART TWO
Small Group Study

Separating Small Groups. Ask the participants to form four small groups. Each group will study a different set of questions and report their findings to the larger group at the end of the study period.

Assign the Bible Application exercises as follows:

Group #1   Defining the Church
Group #2   Traditional Church Models
Group #3   The Church and the Mission of God
Group #4   The Role of the Church

Feel free to tailor the small group study to fit the size and needs of your class. If your study group is small, you may focus on Bible Application exercise #3.

Set a Time Limit. About 15–20 minutes should be sufficient. Check the clock to determine how much time is available. Then notify the groups of the time that they should reconvene.

Sharing Insights. Encourage the small group members to vary their study methods. For example, the participants could locate different verses and take turns reading them aloud to the group. Then they could spend a few minutes discussing the answers to the questions. Or the group could divide the time in half. During the first part they each could read and answer all of the assigned questions. Then they would come together to discuss their answers and share insights and opinions.

Remind them to include a discussion of the Personal Application questions as part of their study.

Preparing Reports. Have each small group select the participant(s) who will take notes, summarize the discussion, and present the group's findings.

Large Group Discussion
Reconvene the Group. Call the small groups back together.

Present Small Group Reports. Have the selected participants report the results of their small group study. Encourage the other groups to take notes, and allow time for discussion and questions within the larger group.

Monitor the Time. Remind the representatives to try to summarize the small group's discussion in two or three minutes. Allocate up to three minutes to discuss each group's presentation.

Going Global Commitment
Read the Going Global exercise aloud to the group. Then give the participants a few minutes to record their opinions. Encourage them to come prepared to share their results next week.

Closing
Ask the participants to read chapter 9 of *Going Global—Beyond the Boundaries* and record their notes at the end of their student workbooks. Remind them to bring their Bibles and workbooks to the next session. Close the class with prayer focused on the lesson aim.

Bible Application Exercises and Answers
1. Defining the Church
Several things may come to mind when we think about the church. However, the thing to remember is that the church is the vehicle through which God has chosen to make Himself known to this generation.

Match the verses below with how the Bible identifies and defines the New Testament church.

     a. Romans 16:5; 1 Corinthians 16:19; Philemon 2
     b. 1 Corinthians 3:16; 6:19; 1 John 4:15
     c. 1 Corinthians 12:27

d. Ephesians 5:25–27
e. 1 Timothy 3:15; 1 Peter 4:17
f. 1 Peter 2:9–10

a a believer's house
e the house of God (the building)
b the temple of God (the believer)
f the people of God
c the body of Christ
d the bride of Christ

Using the definitions above, complete the following sentences by filling in the blanks. (One definition will not be used.)

a. The meeting place in which we gather to worship is often referred to as the **house of God.**

b. The Israelites were originally chosen to be God's people and to witness to the nations. However, through the life, death, and resurrection of Jesus Christ, now all who believe in and follow Him become the **people of God**.

c. The church as the **body of Christ** creates a beautiful picture of believers who work together in unity and diversity to do the work and the will of God on earth.

d. Each believer is the **temple of God** because God's Spirit dwells in us. It is the Spirit of God working through the church that makes us holy and powerful.

e. The church does not belong to the men and women who comprise it. We are members of the church of Jesus Christ and we belong to Him. In all that we do, we must keep in mind that coming day when we will meet the Lord as the **bride of Christ.**

Personal Application
Which definition of the church do you use most often?
Answers will vary.

How does your membership in the body of Christ and your role as the bride of Christ affect your attitudes and actions?
Answers will vary.

2. Traditional Church Models

Three models of the traditional church include: the separational model, the sociological model, and the associational model.

The separational model sought to protect its members from corruption by isolating itself.

    a. Explain how this approach helps our call to missions.
        Answers will vary.

    b. Explain how this approach hinders our call to missions.
        Answers will vary.

The sociological model focused primarily on the social application of the Gospel—often to the neglect of the spiritual.

    a. Explain how this approach helps our call to missions.
        Answers will vary.

    b. Explain how this approach hinders our call to missions.
        Answers will vary.

The associational model focused inward, and centered on encouraging its members to trust God.

    a. Explain how this approach helps our call to missions.
        Answers will vary.

    b. Explain how this approach hinders our call to missions.
        Answers will vary.

Personal Application

How would you describe or classify your church? Explain wh
    Answers will vary.

How could your church increase its effectiveness in both local and foreign missionary efforts?
    Answers will vary.

3. The Church and the Mission of God

God is on a mission. He loves us and wants to restore our relationship with Him and make us His partner in establishing the kingdom of God. As the body of Christ, we must work together to do God's will in this world.

Use the verses below to identify three aspects of God's motivation for missions.

> a. Jeremiah 15:15
>> God is long-suffering toward us because it is His desire that none should perish.

> b. John 3:16; 1 John 4:9–10
>> God loves us.

> c. Romans 8:31–32
>> God wants the best for us.

Use the following verses to identify some promises given to those who show God's love to others.

> a. Matthew 10:42
>> We will be rewarded.

> b. Matthew 25:40
>> It will be counted as ministry to Jesus.

> c. Hebrews 6:10
>> God will not forget it.

Use the following verses to identify how God feels about those who help missionaries.

> a. Matthew 10:40; John 13:20
>> It is like we are helping the Lord.

> b. Matthew 10:41
>> We will share in the worker's reward.

Personal Application
People will know that we are Christians by our love (John 13:34–35; Romans 5:5). List some practical ways that you can show the love of God to those to whom you witness.
> Answers will vary.

The goodness of the Lord can lead men to repentance (Romans 2:4). What good works can you do for those who don't know Christ? How can you pray that God's best will be revealed to those who refuse or reject Him?
　　　Answers will vary.

4. The Role of the Church

Historically, the church has not always functioned in its biblical role. Established by God and called to do a great work for Him, the church has yet to fulfill its divine mandate and potential.

Read the following verses and identify some reasons that the church exists.

　　　a. Ephesians 2:10
　　　　　To do good works

　　　b. Ephesians 3:6
　　　　　To share the Good News with those who are alienated
　　　　　from God

　　　c. Ephesians 3:10
　　　　　To display God's wisdom to evil powers

　　　d. Ephesians 3:20–21
　　　　　To give God glory and praise

According to Ephesians 1:22 and Colossians 1:18, who is the head of the church?
　　　Christ is the head of the church.

Personal Application

Missions originated in the heart of God. It is not an effort to increase church membership. Read Acts 2:47 and 1 Corinthians 3:6–7. What do these Scriptures remind us?
　　　It is the Lord who adds to the church.

Going Global

"Jesus saith unto him, I am the way, the truth, and the life: no man cometh unto the Father, but by me" (John 14:6, KJV). However, many still think that God accepts good people.

How can you communicate the importance of faith in Christ to those who may feel that they don't need the Savior?
　　　Answers will vary.

Chapter 9

New Models of African American Churches

Format for Sessions of 90 Minutes or More

PART ONE		PART TWO	
MIN.	ACTIVITY	MIN.	ACTIVITY
5	Prayer	20	Small Group Study
5	Going Global Discussion	15	Small Group Presentations
5	Chapter Review	15	Large Group Presentations
15	Life Application Discussion	5	Going Global Commitment
20	Life Application Discussion	5	Prayer

For sessions of less than 90 minutes, use PART ONE only and assign the Bible Application exercises as homework. Read the Going Global exercise at the end of the study aloud, and encourage the participants to come prepared to share their results next week. Then close the class in prayer.

*To complete the group study in PART TWO, each participant will need a copy of the student workbook that accompanies the book, *Going Global—Beyond the Boundaries.*

Lesson Aim: At the end of this two-part session, the participants should: (a) identify and describe several new models of African American churches; (b) relate the importance of moving out of the church to impact the world with the Gospel of Jesus Christ; and (c) identify some ways to become more involved in the work of the kingdom.

Key Verse: "But in your hearts set apart Christ as Lord. Always be prepared to give an answer to everyone who asks you to give the reason for the hope that you have. But do this with gentleness and respect" (1 Peter 3:15, NIV).

Lesson Focus: We have a message to share; we have work to do. We must share the Good News of the Gospel through our words and actions. Let us take the love of Christ within us and make a difference in the world around us. It may be the only Gospel that some will ever hear.

PART ONE
Prayer

Open the session with prayer, including the lesson aim.

Going Global Discussion

Invite the participants to share their ideas and opinions related to the Going Global exercise from last week's Bible study.

Introduction

Ask the participants to read the Key Verse aloud in unison. This verse appears at the beginning of chapter 9 in their workbooks. Then ask them to silently read the focus statement that follows this verse. If there are participants who do not have workbooks, read this statement aloud to the group.

Chapter Review

Use the following topics to review and discuss chapter 9.

- Recent Church Models
- The Role of the Church in the World Today

You may write these topics on the chalkboard or newsprint, or uncover them one at a time using an overhead projector and transparencies. Try to limit the discussion to five minutes or less for each topic.

Words You Should Know

It is often useful to define the terms that are discussed to ensure that the group shares a common understanding. Read or display the following definitions and allow a few minutes for questions or comments.

- **Evangelical Model**—A theological outlook focused on private salvation.

- **Charismatic Model**—A theological outlook focused on private salvation and personal spiritual experiences.

- **Prosperity Model**—A theological outlook focused on private salvation and personal well-being.

- **Dominion Model**—A theological outlook focused on impacting society in the name of the kingdom of God.

Life Application Questions

Ask the participants to review and share their answers to the following Life Application questions:

- Identify the theological outlook of your church.
- Does your church have a written statement of faith and a mission statement? If so, what is it? If not, why not?

These Life Application questions also appear in the student workbook with space to record their answers. You can ask the participants to take a few minutes to answer these questions. Or you can read the questions aloud or display them to facilitate discussion. You may also wish to share your point of view as a fellow participant in Bible study.

PART TWO
Small Group Study

Separating Small Groups. Ask the participants to form three small groups. Each group will study a different set of questions and report their findings to the larger group at the end of the study period.

Assign the Bible Application exercises as follows:

Group #1	Theology of the Church
Group #2	The Work of the Church
Group #3	The Church and the Kingdom

Feel free to tailor the small group study to fit the size and needs of your class. If your study group is small, you may focus on Bible Application exercise #3.

Set a Time Limit. About 15–20 minutes should be sufficient. Check the clock to determine how much time is available. Then notify the groups of the time that they should reconvene.

Sharing Insights. Encourage the small group members to vary their study methods. For example, the participants could locate different verses and take turns reading them aloud to the group. Then they could spend a few minutes discussing the answers to the questions. Or the group could divide the time in half. During the first part they each could read and answer all of the assigned questions. Then they would come together to discuss their answers and share insights and opinions. Remind them to include a discussion of the Personal Application questions as part of their study.

Preparing Reports. Have each small group select the participant(s) who will take notes, summarize the discussion, and present the group's findings.

Large Group Discussion

Reconvene the Group. Call the small groups back together.

Present Small Group Reports. Have the selected participants report the results of their small group study. Encourage the other groups to take notes, and allow time for discussion and questions within the larger group.

Monitor the Time. Remind the representatives to try to summarize the small group's discussion in two or three minutes. Allocate up to three minutes to discuss each group's presentation.

Going Global Commitment

Read the Going Global exercise aloud to the group. Encourage them to thoughtfully answer this question during the week.

Closing

Ask the participants to read chapter 10 of *Going Global--Beyond the Boundaries* and record their notes at the end of their student workbooks. Remind them to bring their Bibles and workbooks to the next session. Close the class with prayer focused on the lesson aim.

Bible Application Exercises and Answers

1. Theology of the Church

Like individual believers, the effective church must apply God's Word to every area of life.

Evangelical churches generally focus on the importance of faith in Christ, holy living, Bible study, and prayer.

　　a. Describe the strengths of the evangelical model.
　　　 Answers will vary.

　　b. Describe the weaknesses of the evangelical model.
　　　 Answers will vary.

Charismatic churches usually focus on the gifts of the Spirit, including baptism in the Holy Spirit, speaking in tongues, healing, and prophecy.

a. Describe the strengths of the charismatic model.
    Answers will vary.

b. Describe the weaknesses of the charismatic model.
    Answers will vary.

Prosperity churches generally focus on material and spiritual success.

a. Describe the strengths of the prosperity model.
    Answers will vary.

b. Describe the weaknesses of the prosperity model.
    Answers will vary.

Dominion churches focus on making a difference in the world in the name of the kingdom of God.

a. Describe the strengths of the dominion model.
    Answers will vary.

b. Describe the weaknesses of the dominion model.
    Answers will vary.

Personal Application
Identify the focus and model that characterizes your church.
    Answers will vary.

2. The Work of the Church
We have been called and chosen to accomplish God's purposes. Because of the love of God and our faith in His Son, our Savior, ". . . in this world we are like him" (1 John 4:17).

Match the following verses with some of the reasons that God chose us.

a. Acts 1:8
b. Acts 9:15
c. 1 Corinthians 1:27–29
d. Ephesians 1:4
e. Ephesians 2:10
f. 2 Thessalonians 2:13

b To bear His name
f To receive salvation
e To do good works
c To confound the wise and mighty
d To be holy and blameless
a To be witnesses

The birth of the New Testament church is described in the book of Acts. Read Acts 1:8 and use this verse to answer the following questions.

a. How was the church empowered?
By the Holy Spirit

b. Why was the church empowered?
To be witnesses for Christ

c. Describe the progression or pattern for witnessing.
The pattern is to witness: at home, in the community, in the country, and in the world.

Personal Application
Every believer is on a mission. Jesus said, "As my Father hath sent me, even so send I you" (John 20:21, KJV). Where is God "sending" you to share the Gospel?
Answers will vary.

3. The Church and the Kingdom
The kingdom of God involves more than just the salvation of the church. It is the rule of God and the manifestation of His good, acceptable, and perfect will.

When Jesus taught the disciples to pray, what was their first request (Luke 11:2)?
"Thy kingdom come. Thy will be done, as in heaven, so in earth" (KJV).

Use the following verses to record what the kingdom is not.

a. John 18:36
The kingdom is not of this world; it is not a man-made kingdom.

b. Romans 14:17
The kingdom is not natural, but spiritual.

c. I Corinthians 4:20
   The kingdom is not in word, but in power.

Use the following verses to review the conditions for entry into the kingdom.

a. Mark 1:15
   Repent and believe.

b. Mark 7:21
   Do God's will.

c. John 3:5
   Become born again.

Use the following verses to review the work of the kingdom.

a. Luke 9:2; 10:9
   To heal the sick

b. Acts 4:12; Philippians 2:9–10
   To magnify the name of Jesus

c. I Timothy 1:15
   To save sinners

d. I John 3:8
   To destroy the devil's works.

Personal Application
Describe your current involvement in the work of the kingdom. How can you increase your participation?
   Answers will vary.

Going Global
Look up I Peter 3:15 and write this verse in your own words. Then record your personal testimony beneath this verse. What additional preparation do you need to become ready to witness?
   Answers will vary.

Chapter 10

Let's Get Busy

Format for Sessions of 90 Minutes or More

PART ONE

MIN.	ACTIVITY
5	Prayer
5	Going Global Discussion
5	Introduction
15	Chapter Review
20	Life Application Discussion

PART TWO

MIN.	ACTIVITY
20	Small Group Study
15	Small Group Presentations
15	Large Group Presentations
5	Going Global Commitment
5	Prayer

For sessions of less than 90 minutes, use PART ONE only and assign the Bible Application exercises as homework. Read the Going Global exercise at the end of the study aloud, and encourage the participants to come prepared to share their results next week. Then close the class in prayer.

*To complete the group study in PART TWO, each participant will need a copy of the student workbook that accompanies the book, *Going Global—Beyond the Boundaries.*

Lesson Aim: At the end of this two-part session, the participants should: (a) recognize some of the cultural issues that the church faces today; (b) ask God for His vision and rely upon His power at work in us; and (c) seek to engage the culture in which we live and impact the world with the life giving Gospel of Jesus Christ.

Key Verse: "But whoever drinks the water I give him will never thirst. Indeed, the water I give him will become in him a spring of water welling up to eternal life" (John 4:14, NIV).

Lesson Focus: We must get God's vision for missions. As the African American church follows the example of Jesus Christ, we can impact the racism of ethnic cleansing, decrease the spread of AIDS, improve conditions of poverty, and minister to the spiritual needs of people throughout the world today.

PART ONE
Prayer

Open the session with prayer, including the lesson aim.

Going Global Discussion

Invite the participants to share the testimonies related to the Going Global exercise from last week's Bible study.

Introduction

Ask the participants to read the Key Verse aloud in unison. This verse appears at the beginning of chapter 10 in their workbooks. Then ask them to silently read the focus statement that follows this verse. If there are participants who do not have workbooks, read this statement aloud to the group.

Chapter Review

Use the following topics to review and discuss chapter 10.

- The Divine Significance of the African American Experience
- Cultural Challenges: Materialism, Thug Mentality, and Dysfunctionality
- Re-establishing God-given Dignity, Identity, and Significance
- Rebuilding the Church: A Nehemiah Vision
- Going Global: Impacting the World

You may write these topics on the chalkboard or newsprint, or uncover them one at a time using an overhead projector and transparencies. Try to limit the discussion to five minutes or less for each topic.

Words You Should Know

It is often useful to define the terms that are discussed to ensure that the group shares a common understanding. Read or display the following definitions and allow a few minutes for questions or comments.

- **Thug mentality**—The attitude behind forms of hip-hop and gangsta rap music that embrace early death or imprisonment as consequences of choosing an illegal, immoral, or self-centered lifestyle.

- **Nehemiah**—A man of faith and prayer who saw the trouble and disgrace of his people, and left his high position to lead the task of rebuilding the wall around the city of Jerusalem. Not only did he make a personal sacrifice, he motivated others to help complete the work in 52 days in spite of threats and danger.

- **A Nehemiah Vision**—A refusal to accept things as they are, an understanding of what God wants to be done, and the courage to take action to bring about His desired result.

Life Application Questions

Ask the participants to review and share their answers to the following Life Application questions:

- Why is the vision of the church important?
- Why is the work of the church important?

These Life Application questions also appear in the student workbook with space to record their answers. You can ask the participants to take a few minutes to answer these questions. Or you can read the questions aloud or display them to facilitate discussion. You may also wish to share your point of view as a fellow participant in Bible study.

PART TWO
Small Group Study

Separating Small Groups. Ask the participants to form two groups. Each group will study a different set of questions and report their findings to the larger group at the end of the study period.

Assign the Bible Application exercises as follows:

Group #1   A Chosen Race
Group #2   Out of the Comfort Zone

Feel free to tailor the small group study to fit the size and needs of your class. If your study group is small, you may focus on Bible Application exercise #2.

Set a Time Limit. About 15–20 minutes should be sufficient. Check the clock to determine how much time is available. Then notify the groups of the time that they should reconvene.

Sharing Insights. Encourage the small group members to vary their study methods. For example, the participants could locate different verses and take turns reading them aloud to the group. Then they could spend a few minutes discussing the answers to the questions. Or the group could divide the time in half. During the first part they each could read and answer all of the assigned questions. Then they would come together to discuss their answers and share insights and opinions. Remind them to include a discussion of the Personal Application questions as part of their study.

Preparing Reports. Have each small group select the participant(s) who will take notes, summarize the discussion, and present the group's findings.

Large Group Discussion
Reconvene the Group. Call the small groups back together.

Present Small Group Reports. Have the selected participants report the results of their small group study. Encourage the other groups to take notes, and allow time for discussion and questions within the larger group.

Monitor the Time. Remind the representatives to try to summarize the small group's discussion in two or three minutes. Allocate up to three minutes to discuss each group's presentation.

Going Global Commitment
Read the Going Global exercise aloud to the group. Then give the participants a few minutes to answer the questions and make a personal commitment to do their part to impact the world for the kingdom of God.

Closing
Close the class with prayer focused on the lesson aim.

Bible Application Exercises and Answers
1. A Chosen Race
Our God–given identity is directly connected with our destiny. We have been called and chosen to accomplish God's purposes.

Read 1 Peter 2:9. Then rewrite this verse below as a series of personal statements. Begin with: "I am a member of a . . . ."
     Answers will vary.

According to this verse, why have we been selected, valued, sanctified, and set apart by God in love?
     To show forth His praises.

Read Philippians 2:12–13. Rewrite these verses in your own words. Then describe what this truth means to you.

Answers will vary.

Personal Application

Only what you do for Christ will last. List some things that you are doing that will count for the glory of God. Or if necessary, identify some things that you can begin to do.

Answers will vary.

2. Out of the Comfort Zone

We cannot be saved and satisfied. We must become like Nehemiah and get a vision of the work that God has called us to do. God has given us the power to do His will.

Read Matthew 5:13–17. Use this passage to answer the following questions.

  a. Why do you think these two metaphors are used to describe the role of the believer in society?

  Light conquers the darkness; salt is a preservative that prevents decay.

  b. Describe what will happen if we do not fulfill this role in our culture?

  Darkness and death will prevail.

  c. Identify some actions the church can take to do this work.

  Answers will vary.

  d. Identify two specific things that you can do.

  Answers will vary.

Read John 15:5–8, 16. Use this passage to answer the following questions.

  a. Why do you think this metaphor is used to describe our relationship to Christ?

  Because our spiritual life flows from our belief and trust in Him.

  b. Why do we have this relationship?

  So that we can bear spiritual fruit and glorify God.

c. Identify some things that you can do to sustain or increase your connection to Christ.
>Answers will vary.

Read 2 Corinthians 3:2-3. Use these verses to answer the following questions.

a. Why do you think this metaphor is used to describe the role of believer in society?
>It has been said that we are the only Bible some people will ever read.

b. Describe what will happen if we do not fulfill this role in our culture?
>People may not understand how God's love can make a difference in a person's heart and life.

c. Identify one thing that you can do to show someone the reality of Christ.
>Answers will vary.

Read 2 Corinthians 5:20. Use this verse to answer the following questions.

a. Why do you think this metaphor is used to describe the role of believer in society?
>We represent Christ in the world today.

b. Describe what will happen if we do not fulfill this role in our culture?
>People may not hear the message of the Gospel or see God's love in action.

c. Identify two practical things that you can do to represent Christ to someone around you this week.
>Answers will vary.

Read 2 Corinthians 10:3-4. Use this passage to answer the following questions.

a. What kind of weapons do we have?
>Mighty spiritual weapons

b. What work do we use them to accomplish?
>The pulling down of strongholds.

c. List some of the things that you think are included in the believer's arsenal.

> Answers will vary. They may include love, the Word of God, and prayer.

God loves people. Read Ephesians 6:12 to identify who or what we are fighting against.

> We are fighting against spiritual wickedness.

What does 2 Timothy 2:3–4 and 1 Thessalonians 2:4 reveal about our purpose as soldiers of Christ?

> Our purpose is to please the Lord.

Going Global

Evaluate your outreach efforts. On a scale of 1–10, rate the following:

- Your support of national or international missions/outreach programs
- Your participation in the work of local evangelism
- How often you share your testimony
- How often you acknowledge God in your conversation with others
  > Answers will vary.

Jesus said, "But whosoever drinketh of the water that I shall give him shall never thirst; but the water that I shall give him shall be in him a well of water springing up into everlasting life" (John 4:14, KJV). Yet, each day millions die and go to an eternity without Christ.

The time is short. As people who have been given the power of God unto salvation (Romans 1:16), let's do our part to impact the world for the kingdom of God by:

- Being who we are—"'*You are my witnesses,' declares the LORD*" (Isaiah 43:10; cf. Acts 1:8).

- Sharing what we have—"*Silver and gold I do not have, but what I have I give you*" (Acts 3:6).

- Serving those to whom God sends us—"*Again Jesus said, 'Peace be with you! As the Father has sent me, I am sending you'*" (John 20:21).

- Remembering that we do not work alone—"*And surely I am with you always, to the very end of the age*" (Matthew 28:20).

History of UMI (Urban Ministries, Inc.)

The establishment of UMI (Urban Ministries, Inc.) was the fulfillment of a boyhood dream that Melvin E. Banks had at the age of 12. Soon after accepting Jesus Christ as his Savior, young Melvin gave his testimony on one of the back roads of Birmingham, Alabama. An old, white-haired Black man heard Melvin's testimony and quoted this verse to him: "My people are destroyed for lack of knowledge" (Hosea 4:6, KJV). This verse made a great impression on Melvin, and he was determined to yield himself to God so that he could be used to help bring the knowledge of His Word to Black people.

While working at Scripture Press, Melvin realized the need for resources that would appeal to urban Black Christians. In 1970, the Board of Directors was selected and Melvin's boyhood dream began to take shape with the incorporation of UMI.

During its first 12 years, UMI operated out of the basement of the Banks home. In 1982, UMI occupied the second floor of 1439 West 103rd Street in Chicago, Illinois. In 1985, UMI expanded its operation to include the first floor. In 1990, UMI moved to 1350 West 103rd Street in Chicago. In the spring of 1996, UMI completed construction and took occupancy of a new 21,000 square foot headquarters in the Chicagoland area.

The vision of a company, where committed Christians can devote themselves to the preparation of Christ-centered resources, continues to grow as UMI ministers to African Americans. The company is challenged to reach every Black Christian church with Christian education products and services. In accomplishing this mission, UMI recognizes its responsibility to our Lord, employees, customers, the community, and society.

Prayer Requests

_____

_____

_____

_____

_____

_____

_____

_____

_____

_____

_____

_____

_____

_____

_____

_____

_____